The Crafty Witch

The Crafty Witch

101 Ideas

for Every Occasion

WILLOW POLSON

CITADEL PRESS
Kensington Publishing Corp.
www.kensingtonbooks.com

CITADEL PRESS BOOKS are published by

Kensington Publishing Corp.
850 Third Avenue
New York, NY 10022

All Kensington titles, imprints, and distributed lines are available at special quantity
discounts for bulk purchases for sales promotions, premiums, fund-raising, educational, or
institutional use. Special book excerpts or customized printings can also be created to fit specific
needs. For details, write or phone the office of the Kensington special sales manager: Kensington
Publishing Corp., 850 Third Avenue, New York, NY 10022, attn: Special Sales Department,
phone 1-800-221-2647.

CITADEL PRESS and the Citadel logo are Reg. U.S. Pat. & TM Off.

Book design by Anne Ricigliano

First printing: September 2007

10 9 8 7 6 5 4 3 2 1

Printed in the United States of America

Library of Congress Control Number: 2007928705

ISBN-13: 978-0-8065-2678-2
ISBN-10: 0-8065-2678-5

To my fans and friends around the world,

and to the Old Ones who find subtle ways

to inspire us every moment of our lives.

Honor them as they honor you

with the gift of creativity.

Contents

Introduction

Ever since *Witch Crafts* made its debut in November 2001, people have been asking me when will my next book of Pagan craft projects be available. I'm pleased to present you with that very book!

For those who haven't read my first book, this volume repeats some facts such as basic craft techniques or company contact information in the Resources at the end of each chapter. I've tried, however, to repeat as little as possible and to introduce new companies when appropriate to keep the chapters fresh. Another fresh thing you'll discover are many new materials and techniques, and the chapters are arranged a little differently to accommodate these and to organize the projects properly.

I received some negative *Witch Crafts* reviews from some because of the "Fauna" chapter, so let me warn you that, yes, there is another Fauna chapter here (meaning crafts made from leather or other animal parts). As a vegetarian myself it seems contradictory to include projects of this nature here, but remember that our ancestors used every part of the animals they hunted or farmed, such as the quills of the porcupine, leather from the animal skins, and the rattles from rattlesnakes. Sometimes these were important parts of folk remedies, Native American medicine bags, or magic spells, so I've chosen to again include in this book projects that use these materials.

Speaking of magic, last time I talked a bit about adding intent to your crafts as you work. Ways to do this range from simple working chants to elaborate rituals. The repetitive chants work best when done with a repetitive task, such as crochet, cross-stitch, or knitting. If the piece is particularly meaningful to you, a good way to start is to bathe and purify yourself, then do the craft inside your sacred space.

At my local Pagan Pride Day a couple of years ago I talked a bit about how creativity is a two-way street between you and the Divine. You receive inspiration from Divinity, and in turn Divinity is honored when you create things of beauty. And you don't have to make something specifically religious in nature—handcrafting an afghan for your sister's baby shower is just as wonderful as embroidering an altar cloth with your deity's image on it. Whether the finished product is sacred or not, your ability to make something with your own hands from raw materials is a gift to be recognized and honored.

Creativity seems to be such a natural in the Pagan community—we're a feeling people and we love to work with our hands. Creativity can go beyond making craft projects; it appears in every facet of our community from ritual theater to the bardic arts, from cooking holiday foods to finding a new way for a coven to celebrate. If you feel that "I can't make things, I'm not creative," don't believe it for a moment. Everyone is creative in his or her own way, and if you know this to be true in your heart and are willing to try new things, you may surprise yourself with some of the projects in this book!

The projects are arranged (generally) by difficulty level, with the easier projects listed first and the harder ones near the end of the chapter. Of course, this is purely subjective—some people freak out when they see French knots in an embroidery design and would categorize the project as "difficult," while others think this is the easiest stitch in the universe and have no trouble making it. Read through the projects and directions before deciding which one to make first, based on your skill level and access to needed supplies. Some crafts may require really good eyesight (or a magnifying lamp); some may aggravate your carpal tunnel syndrome; some involve animal products; and some may involve substances that make your allergies flare up. Only you can decide if a project is right for you.

Try something new, revel in something familiar, make something wonderful! I look forward to hearing from you and seeing photos of your completed project. Share it with your circle-mates, your kids, your friends, and anyone else who loves to create special things for ritual and for the home. This book is for you.

Acknowledgments

As always, I give heartfelt thanks to my husband Craig for being so supportive and encouraging—without him I would not have completed this book. A huge thanks also to my patient and generous craft project designers and model makers—Leora, Sierra, Denise, Glenda, Karen, Melissa, Kristal, Pat and others. Thanks also to my mentors and editors—Danielle Chotti for her patience with me, Bob Shuman for kindly putting up with my late additions, Margaret Wolf for seeing me through some rough times and having a wicked sense of humor, and Judy Swager for being an awesome editor when I first started. A special thanks to my little boy Cian for letting me work when I needed to, even when you wanted me to play. Now that the book is finally done I can!

And where would I be without all my suppliers! Long live the independent craft supply shops around the world! Please support these small businesses, either in your town or on the Internet.

The Crafty Witch

Charted Needlework

The nice thing about charted needlework is that someone else has done the hardest bit for you—designing the pattern. The two most common types of charted needlework are cross stitch and needlepoint, and even these simple techniques have variations beyond the basic "square on chart equals stitch" idea.

Cross-stitch, because of its nature as a primarily pictorial medium, usually creates the image with simple square stitches augmented by half and quarter stitches. A variation of cross-stitch is Assisi work, which is said to have originated with a nun at the convent of St. Francis in Assisi, Italy. It's basically cross-stitch with backstitched outlines, but the design is created by the fabric negative space left between the colorful stitched areas rather than the other way around.

Needlepoint has a wide variety of specialty stitches, especially used in backgrounds and to create interesting texture where single stitches seem too ordinary. Breaking away from the sturdy single-stitch needlepoint used to create chair cushions and so on, canvaswork adds a host of lacy, overlapping, and difficult stitches while still remaining in the "charted" category, but in this chapter I've kept things simple by using primarily basic cross-stitch and needlepoint techniques with only one simple specialty stitch found in the background of the Needlepoint Sacred Lotus.

Since the stitches are simple for the most part, you can have fun with the interesting metallic fibers used in this chapter. I'm a big fan of Kreinik metallics and use them extensively in many of my projects for that shimmery bit of magic that would be missing if you used plain cotton floss. Of course, you're free to substitute fibers and colors as you like in any of the projects (but you need to send me a picture!) and have fun with the different effects gained by experimentation.

A word about colorfastness, and this applies to all the needlework fibers used throughout this book: due to recent governmental regulations, no longer can fibers be guaranteed as colorfast. Thus, you need to test your fibers before stitching with them, especially if you plan to use them on a garment or other article that will be washed frequently. To do this, wet the threads and then put them between a fold of white cloth. Iron on hot, and see if any color comes away on the white cloth. If it bleeds badly, you can try using a vinegar soak in hot water to set the color in the skein before stitching with it, but chances are this will have limited success. If you must wash your finished work, carefully squeeze it in cold water using baby shampoo or heirloom quilt soap, rinse in cold water briefly, and dry it flat on stretcher bars without ironing unless you know the colors will not bleed.

Generally, it has been my experience that most cotton floss is very colorfast as are the Kreinik metallics. Also, with the exception of the Sabbat Towel, none of the projects in this book are designed to be washed in a machine. So, unless they've become soiled while being stitched, don't worry about colorfastness. Simply follow the chart and enjoy the colorful results.

CROSS-STITCH "NEVER THIRST" SIPPIE CUP

Wish a special little one well with this magical sippie cup that really delivers on its message! Happy water droplets will bring a smile to a child's face as he or she takes a drink. The message is also "public friendly" enough to take anywhere without causing a stir. Model stitched by Patricia Bennett.

YOU'LL NEED:

Charles Craft E-Z Stitch Sippie Cup (your choice of color;
    white or blue would work best)
DMC floss, 1 skein each:
    825—blue, dark
    827—blue, very light
    910—emerald green, dark
    3818—emerald green, ultra very dark
#5 embroidery needle or your favorite cross-stitch needle
Scissors

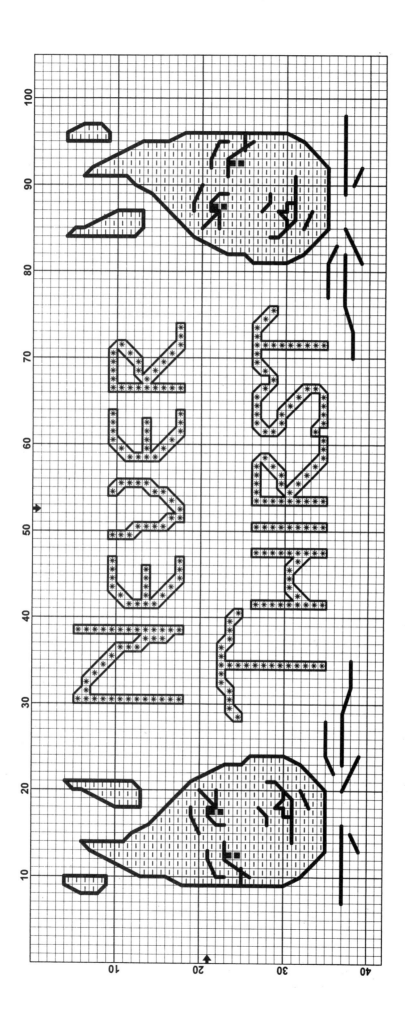

3

Fabric:	Premade Sippie Cup Insert 14, White
	91w × 35h Stitches
Size:	14 Count, 6-1/2w × 2-1/2h

Floss Used for Full Stitches:

Symbol	Strands	Type	Number	Color
■	3	DMC	825	Blue—DK
−	3	DMC	827	Blue—VY LT
*	3	DMC	910	Emerald Green—DK

Floss Used for Back Stitches:

Symbol	Strands	Type	Number	Color
——	3	DMC	825	Blue—VY LT
——	3	DMC	3818	Emerald Green—UL VY DK

Remove the plastic canvas insert from the sippie cup. Following the chart, center the design and work the cross-stitches (3 strands), then the backstitching as shown (2 strands). Replace the insert and snap the lid in place.

CROSS-STITCH "WITCH'S BREW" MUG

What do Witches drink first thing in the morning? You guessed it . . . and you can enjoy it even more in this whimsical cup accompanied by a cute little black cat peeping over a magical cauldron full of your favorite beverage. Model stitched by Loretta Oliver.

YOU'LL NEED:

Charles Craft E-Z Stitch Coffee Mug
DMC floss, 1 skein each:
    310—black
    435—brown, very light
    552—violet, medium
    645—beaver grey, very dark
    702—kelly green
    844—beaver brown, ultra dark
    907—parrot green, light

The Crafty Witch

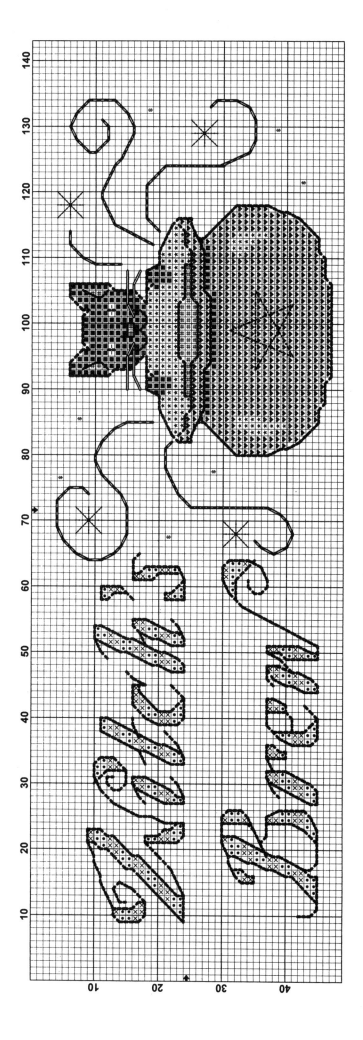

5

Kreinik cord—105C antique silver
Kreinik Japan #5—001J silver and 002J gold
#5 embroidery needle or your favorite cross stitch needle
Scissors

Fabric:	Premade Mug Insert 14, White
	125w × 43h Stitches
Size:	14 Count, 8-7/8w × 3h

Floss Used for Full Stitches:

Symbol	Strands	Type	Number	Color
★	3	DMC	169	Pewter–LT
■	3	DMC	310	Black
#	3	DMC	435	Brown–VY LT
•	3	DMC	552	Violet–MD
♥	3	DMC	645	Beaver Gray–VY DK
×	3	DMC	702	Kelly Green—VY DK
−	3	DMC	907	Parrot Green—LT
$	1	K Japan #5	002J	Gold

Floss Used for Back Stitches:

Symbol	Strands	Type	Number	Color
▬▬▬▬	2	DMC	310	Black
▬▬▬	2	DMC	435	Brown–VY LT
▬▬▬	2	DMC	645	Beaver Gray–VY DK
▬▬▬	1	K Cord	105C	Antique Silver

Floss Used for Straight Stitches:

Symbol	Strands	Type	Number	Color
—·—·—	1	K Japan #5	001J	Silver
·——·——·	1	K Japan #5	002J	Gold

Remove the plastic canvas insert from the mug. Following the chart, center the design and work the cross-stitches (3 strands), then the back-stitching (2 strands) as shown, working the cord (1 strand) and Japan #5 (1 strand) last. Replace the insert and snap the lid in place.

The Crafty Witch

CROSS-STITCH "WHEEL OF THE YEAR" SABBAT TOWEL

This festive holiday guest towel isn't for just once a year, then stored in a box the rest of the time—with a cheerful "Merry Sabbat" greeting, you can use it all year long and delight your special guests. Model stitched by Alice Pace.

YOU'LL NEED:

Charles Craft velour fingertip towel, seafoam or ecru

DMC floss, 1 skein each:
- 111—variegated brown
- 433—brown, medium
- 909—emerald green, very dark
- 911—emerald green, medium
- 3782—mocha brown, light

#5 embroidery needle or your favorite cross-stitch needle

Scissors

Following the chart, start at the center of the design and work the cross-stitches first (3 strands). For the blended browns of the wooden wheel, combine one strand of each color in the needle for a "tweed" effect as you stitch. Work the backstitching last.

Fabric:	Premade Fingertip Towel 14, Seafoam
	90w × 27h Stitches
Size:	14 Count, 6³⁄₈w × 1⁷⁄₈h

Floss Used for Full Stitches:

Symbol	Strands	Type	Number	Color
●	3	DMC	911	Emerald Green–MD
	1	DMC	111	
×	1	DMC	3782	Mocha Brown–LT
	1	DMC	433	Brown–MD

Floss Used for Quarter Stitches:

Symbol	Strands	Type	Number	Color
●	3	DMC	911	Emerald Green–MD
	1	DMC	111	
×	1	DMC	3782	Mocha Brown–LT
	1	DMC	433	Brown–MD

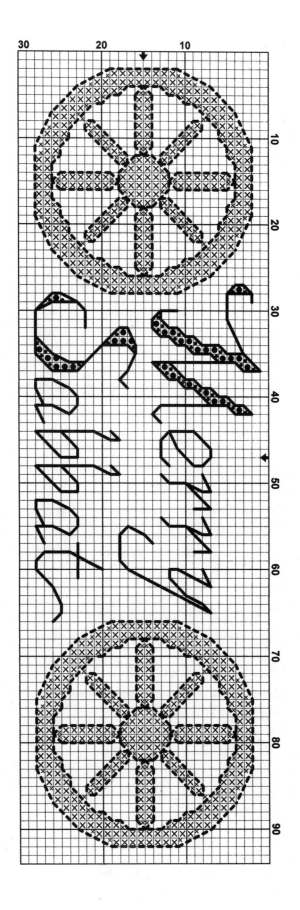

continued from page 7

Floss Used for Straight Stitches:

Symbol	Strands	Type	Number	Color
– – –	2	DMC	433	Brown–MD
——	2	DMC	909	Emerald Green–VY DK

"MAGIC IN PROGRESS" DOOR HANGER

Many people have a separate area for their personal sacred space, whether you have the luxury of an entire ritual room set aside in your home or you're a teen whose whole world is inside your bedroom. This handy and durable sign lets people know not to disturb you, whether you're peacefully meditating or whipping up a powerful spell. Model stitched by Kim Mattox.

YOU'LL NEED:

> Darice 14-count perforated plastic canvas,
>   8¼-inch × 11-inch sheet, clear or white
> DMC floss, 1 skein each:
>   310—black
>   434—brown, light
> Kreinik #4 Very Fine Braid—102 Vatican, 002J Japan gold
> Kreinik Cord—202C indigo
> Needle Necessities metallic braid—4083 Jewels of the Nile
> #5 embroidery needle or your favorite cross-stitch needle
> Scissors

Stitch the design as charted first, before cutting the doorhanger shape, to avoid snagging your threads. Use two strands of floss and one strand of all the metallics. When you're done with the design, carefully cut out the doorhanger shape as shown by the thick black lines on the pattern. If you prefer, you can enlarge the pattern to size and use a permanent marker to mark out the curved shape before cutting. Use the black floss to satin-stitch around all the edges to soften them if you like.

Fabric:	Perforated Plastic 14, White
	84w × 153h Stitches
Size:	14 Count, 6w × 10⁷⁄₈h in

Floss Used for Full Stitches:

Symbol	Strands	Type	Number	Color
■	2	DMC	310	Black
♥	2	DMC	434	Brown–LT
◣	1	Cust Thrd	4083	NN #4 Metallic Braid, Jewels of the Nile

Floss Used for Back Stitches:

Symbol	Strands	Type	Number	Color
	2	DMC	310	Black

Floss Used for Straight Stitches:

Symbol	Strands	Type	Number	Color
▬▬▬	1	K Braid #4	102	Vatican Gold
– – –	1	K Braid #4	002J	Gold (JT)
——	1	K Cord	202C	Indigo

ASSISI CANDLE HUGGER

This project can be altered to fit almost any size of pillar candle by shortening or lengthening the back section. The simple Assisi stitching forms a striking monochromatic design that can be stitched in any color you choose, with or without backstitching. It also features a handy Velcro closure for a snug fit around your candles.

YOU'LL NEED:

1 package Bucilla Ribband, 1⁷⁄₈-inch wide, ecru
Pillar candle
Scissors
1-inch length white or ecru hook-and-loop tape
Ecru sewing thread and sewing machine
Needle Necessities overdyed floss—1421 Snoqualmie Falls
DMC floss—310 black (optional)
#5 embroidery needle or your favorite cross-stitch needle

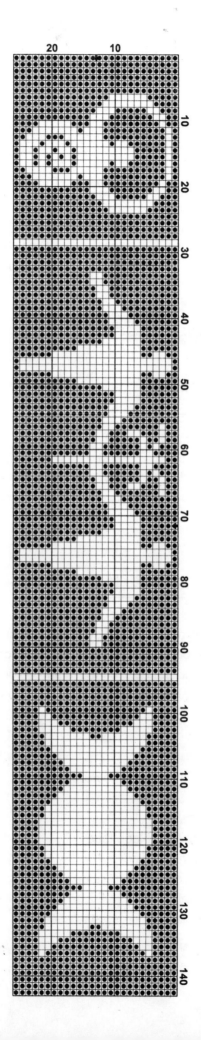

12

Fabric:	Bucilla Ribband Aida 14, White
	143w × 26h Stitches
Size:	14 Count, 10$\frac{1}{8}$w × 1$\frac{3}{4}$h in

Floss Used for Full Stitches:

Symbol	Strands	Type	Number	Color
●	2	NN Floss	OD 1421	Snoqualmie Falls

Wrap the Ribband around your pillar candle, leave about 1$\frac{3}{4}$-inch over-lap on both halves, and cut the Ribband to length. Fold over the ends of the Ribband about $\frac{1}{2}$-inch on each end so that the ends overlap at the back of the candle. Separate the halves of the hook-and-loop tape and stitch the halves to the ends of the Ribband.

Choose one of the charted motifs and center it at the front of the Rib-band. If it's easier for you, photocopy and tape together multiples of the same motif to get the proper spacing between them rather than counting. It looks nicer to repeat the same motif rather than mixing them on the same band. Stitch as charted using 3 strands of floss for good color coverage. You can either stop at this point or add black backstitching around the designs as charted.

NEEDLEPOINT SACRED LOTUS

Designed in two colorways, this project can be finished as a meditation cushion, prayer kneeler, or simply a beautiful accent pillow. The blue lotus is sacred in ancient Egypt as the source of Atum the creator and the symbol of holy perfume, while the pink lotus is sacred in India and Asia where it represents purity, divinity, fertility, and beauty.

YOU'LL NEED:

DMC tapestry wool:
- 7042—kelly green (1 skein)
- 7043—bright green (8 skeins)
- 7435—canary yellow deep (1 skein)
- 7436—tangerine light (1 skein)

Blue variation:
- 7018—cornflower blue very light (4 skeins)
- 7020—cornflower blue dark (2 skeins)
- 7021—blue violet very light (2 skeins)
- 7032—blue violet medium light (2 skeins)

Pink variation:
- 7003—dusty rose very light (4 skeins)
- 7004—carnation very light (2 skeins)
- 7005—carnation light (2 skeins)
- 7191—peach very light (2 skeins)

Paternayan wool—#7 variegated teal (110 yards)
#18 blunt tapestry needle
Scissors
Stretcher bars slightly larger than your finished work
Rustproof tacks or staples

Begin in the center of the design and work your way out. This is a large design, so starting in the middle will help minimize canvas distortion, as will using the basketweave stitch as charted. The DMC yarn usage given is calculated for this stitch. For very small areas, a simple tent stitch is fine to use, but be sure to use basketweave in the larger color areas. The background is done in Double Chevron Wave to suggest rippling water and is faster to work up than the basketweave, as well as adding interest and texture to your piece. The Paternayan yarn usage given is calculated for this stitch.

When all stitching is completed, dampen it and correct the canvas distortion as you attach it to the stretcher bars so that when it dries it will be blocked into a perfect square. Finish it as desired, either as a pillow, thick cushion, or even a framed piece.

Fabric:	Mono canvas 14, White
	170w × 170h Stitches
Size:	14 Count, 12$\frac{1}{8}$w × 12$\frac{1}{8}$h in

Floss Used for Full Stitches:

Symbol	Strands	Type	Number	Color
∞	2	Cust Thrd	7	Paternayan Variegated Wool
+	1	Cust Thrd	7018	DMC Laine Colbert Tapestry Wool
●	1	Cust Thrd	7020	DMC Laine Colbert Tapestry Wool
○	1	Cust Thrd	7021	DMC Laine Colbert Tapestry Wool
▼	1	Cust Thrd	7032	DMC Laine Colbert Tapestry Wool
×	1	Cust Thrd	7042	DMC Laine Colbert Tapestry Wool
╱	1	Cust Thrd	7043	DMC Laine Colbert Tapestry Wool
∴	1	Cust Thrd	7035	DMC Laine Colbert Tapestry Wool
★	1	Cust Thrd	7036	DMC Laine Colbert Tapestry Wool

Blue needlepoint

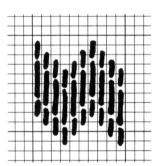

Double Chevron Stitch

Fabric:	Mono canvas 14, White
	170w × 170h Stitches
Size:	14 Count, 12⅛w × 12⅛h in

Floss Used for Full Stitches:

Symbol	Strands	Type	Number	Color
∞	2	Cust Thrd	7	Paternayan Variegated Wool
✚	2	Cust Thrd	7018	DMC Laine Colbert Tapestry Wool
●	2	Cust Thrd	7020	DMC Laine Colbert Tapestry Wool
○	2	Cust Thrd	7021	DMC Laine Colbert Tapestry Wool
▼	2	Cust Thrd	7032	DMC Laine Colbert Tapestry Wool
×	2	Cust Thrd	7042	DMC Laine Colbert Tapestry Wool
╱	2	Cust Thrd	7043	DMC Laine Colbert Tapestry Wool
∴	2	Cust Thrd	7035	DMC Laine Colbert Tapestry Wool
★	2	Cust Thrd	7036	DMC Laine Colbert Tapestry Wool

Pink needlepoint

The Crafty Witch

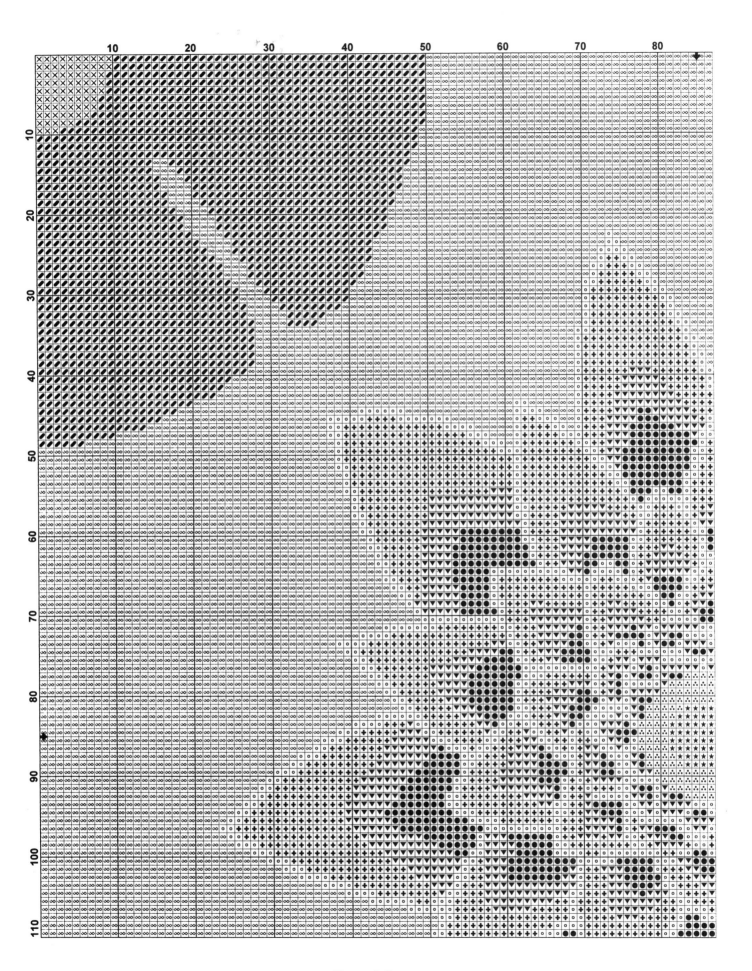

Upper left corner

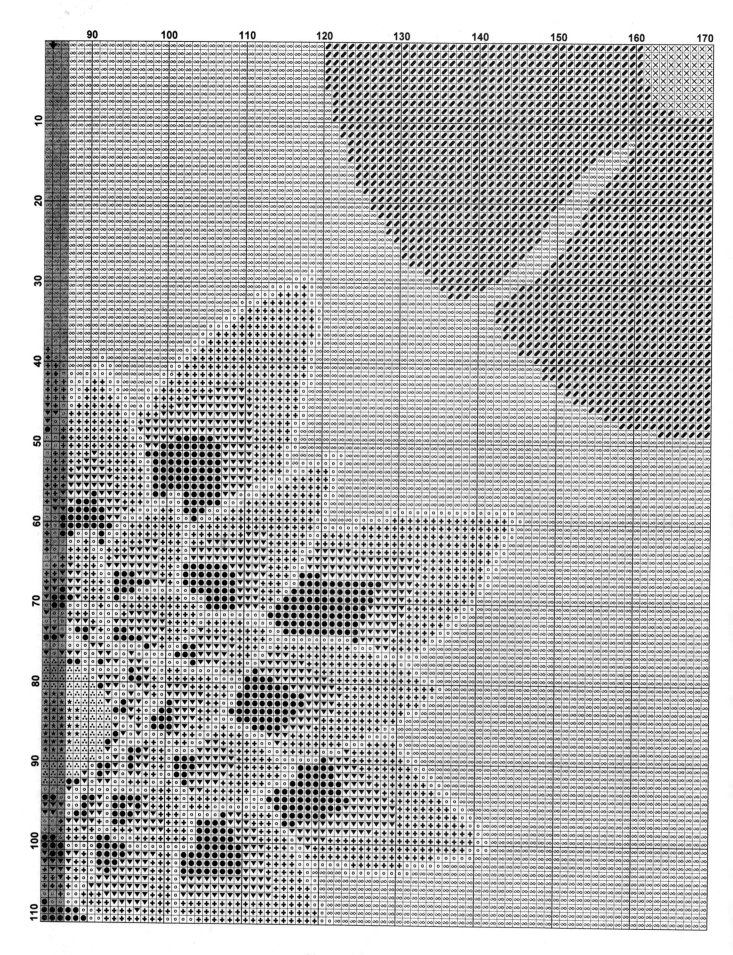

Upper right corner

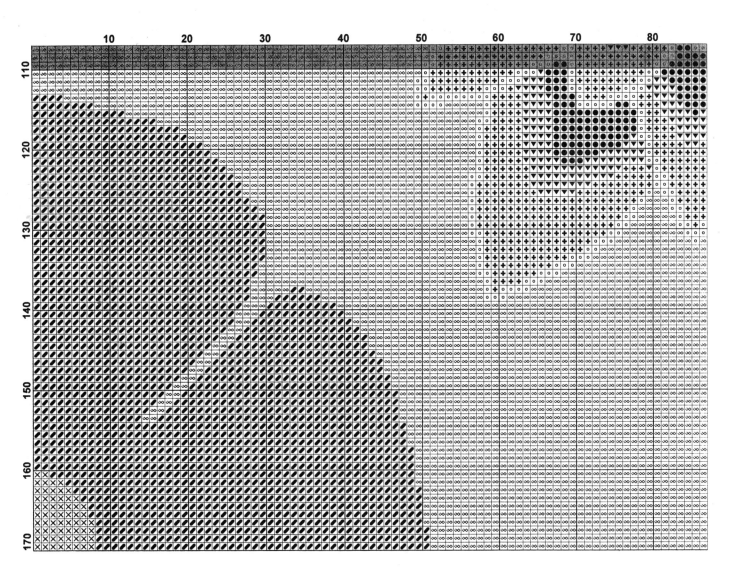

Lower left corner

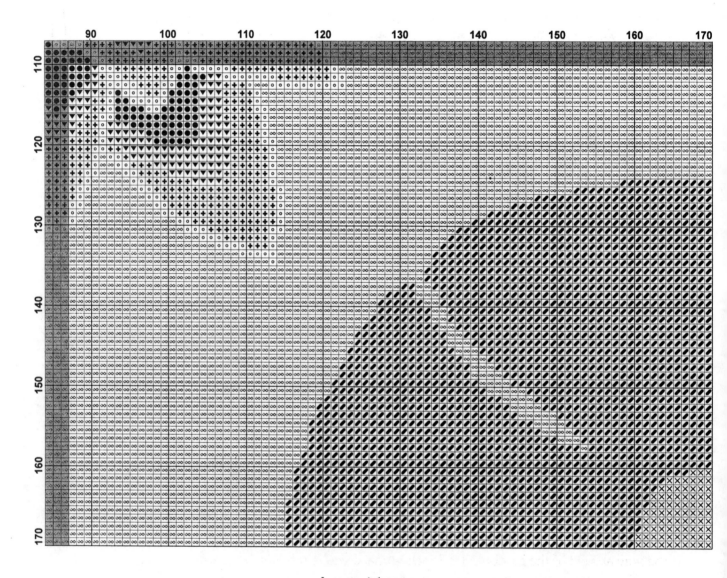

Lower right corner

CROSS-STITCH CHINESE GOOD LUCK HANGER

Yes, this project is upside down! In traditional Chinese culture if you hang this lucky sign upside down you'll be blessed with double the luck, so be sure to get it the right (or wrong) way up when you finish it. The red represents good fortune and happiness, and gold represents wealth, so this design is perfect for the positive feng shui atmosphere in your home or office.

YOU'LL NEED:

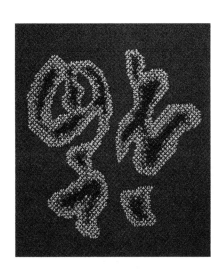

12-inch square of 14 count aida, red
Kreinik #8 fine braid:
    002—Japan gold
    003HL—red high luster
    203—flame
#5 embroidery needle or your choice
Scissors
6-inch or 7-inch square of acid-free cardboard or chipboard
Large piece of cardboard, blank paper, etc., for spraying on
Archival spray-mount adhesive
8-inch square of red fabric
Tacky craft glue
1 yard of metallic gold cord
1 metallic gold tassel
Glue gun and glue sticks

Stitch the design as charted, starting in the center of the design and working your way out. It can also be helpful to start with a red section and work out from there, building the Chinese characters outward as you go. Trim the finished needlework fabric to ½-inch larger than the cardboard all the way around (if the cardboard is 7 inches, make your cloth 8-inch square).

Spray the cardboard on one side with the spray-mount adhesive and allow to set according to the directions on the can. Lightly spray the back of your finished embroidery and carefully center the sticky side of the cardboard over the stitched area, gently but firmly pressing it down so that they are fully adhered. Immediately check for center and reposition if needed before the glue fully bonds. Fold the rough edges of the fabric under so that it's even with the edges of the cardboard. Use a tiny bit of craft glue in the corners if necessary.

Spray the cardboard backing of your stitched piece, and also spray the square of red fabric. Lay the red fabric over the square and smooth in place,

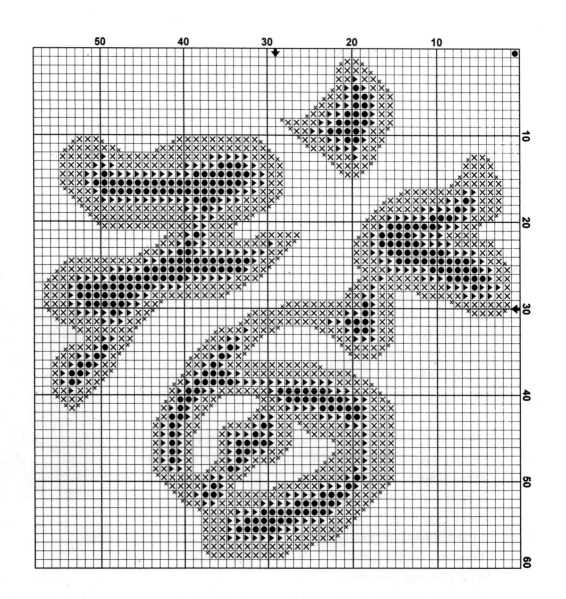

Fabric:	Aida 14, Red
	59w × 57h Stitches
Size:	14 Count, 4¹/₈w × 4h in

Floss Used for Full Stitches:

Symbol	Strands	Type	Number	Color
▲	2	K Braid #8	203	Flame Special Blend
×	2	K Braid #8	002J	Gold (JT)
●	2	K Braid #8	003HL	Red Hi Lustre

Floss Used for Quarter Stitches:

Symbol	Strands	Type	Number	Color
×	2	K Braid #8	002J	Gold (JT)

folding the four rough sides under so that they match the cardboard square. Use a bit of craft glue in the corners if necessary. You should now have a needlework-cardboard-red fabric sandwich.

In the center of the gold cord, tie a knot to make a hanging loop. Set this knot at the top of the cardboard sandwich diamond and attach with the glue gun. Working your way down both sides, glue the cord down. When you reach the bottom, trim the ends to match and glue down well. Attach the gold tassel at the bottom corner.

TRIQUETERA PETIT-POINT BUTTON EARRINGS

Delicate triangular knots accented with gold form these creative earrings made from fabric-covered buttons. The silvery metal base shows through the fabric just enough to lend a subtle shimmer to the overall design. You'll get a lot of compliments from these unusual accessories.

YOU'LL NEED:

32-count linen or evenweave
DMC floss, 1 skein each:
   319—pistachio green, very dark
   988—forest green, medium
Kreinik #4 Very Fine Braid—002J Japan gold
Scissors
#5 embroidery needle
$7/8$-inch, 2-part rust-proof flat buttons for covering with fabric
Needle-nose pliers
Scrap of heavy cardstock paper
Surgical steel earring posts and nuts
Extra-strong tacky craft glue, hot glue, or jeweler's epoxy

Stitch the design as charted, then trim the fabric into a circle, following the pattern on the button package. Be sure your embroidery is centered in the circle. With the pliers, remove the button shank wire from inside the button front section. Carefully lay the fabric over the button blank and catch the fabric in the back hooks, pressing and adjusting it until your design is centered, the front is smooth, and there are no large folds along the back edge.

Cut a small circle of cardstock to match the inside circle of the button back. Put an earring post through the slot, slide it to one end of the slot, and glue it in place, using the cardstock as a backing. The card will help hold the post in place and prevent anything from getting inside the hollow earring.

Fabric:	Linen 32, Mushroom
	19w × 20h Stitches
Size:	32 Count, 0¹/₂w × 0⁵/₈h in

Floss Used for Full Stitches:

Symbol	Strands	Type	Number	Color
●	2	DMC	319	Pistachio Green–VY DK
×	2	DMC	988	Forest Green–MD
■	2	K Braid #4	002J	Gold (JT)

Floss Used for Back Stitches:

Symbol	Strands	Type	Number	Color
——	1	DMC	319	Pistachio Green–VY DK

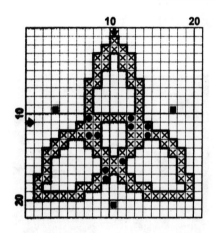

When the glue is completely cured and/or dry, align the back of the earring with the front and snap it in place. Make sure the slot of the button back runs vertical to the design so that the post is closer to the top of the button. This will help the earrings sit correctly when worn.

RESOURCES

Charles Craft, Inc.
P.O. Box 1049
Laurinburg, NC 28353
(910) 844-3521; www.charlescraft.com

One of the premier manufacturers of prefinished cross-stitch supplies, such as towels, cups, baby items, and more. They're also one of the best-selling cross-stitch fabric suppliers and easily found in most craft stores.

The Cottage Discount Needlework
P.O. Box 864691
Plano, TX 75023
(888) 227-9988; www.discountneedlework.com

One of the only places to get Paternayan wool, and a great general needlework supply resource.

Kreinik Mfg. Co., Inc.
3106 Lord Baltimore Drive, Suite 101
Baltimore, MD 21244
(800) 537-2166; www.kreinik.com

Kreinik is the top supplier of metallic fibers for all kinds of needlework. Whether you need extra-fine metallic blending fibers, high-quality Japan threads, or shimmery variegated stitching braids, choose Kreinik.

Nordic Needle, Inc.
1314 Gateway Drive SW
Fargo, ND 58103
(800) 433-4321; www.nordicneedle.com

Just about any kind of needlework fiber and book you could possibly want! An amazing selection of materials for the serious stitcher.

2

Surface Embroidery

As its name implies, the category of "surface embroidery" involves the embellishment of the fabric's surface using various methods of embroidery. Rather than the more static, blocky look achieved with charted designs such as cross- stitch and needlepoint, the freeform nature of surface embroidery is a world without borders—anything goes, and it goes anywhere you like. Flowing lines, naturalistic images, and three-dimensional texture are the hall-marks of this family of needlework techniques.

Different materials are normally used as well. While you can use 7-mm ribbons on needlepoint canvas or Japan gold for cross-stitch, this is not their most effective use and not what they were created to do. Some forms of surface embroidery use materials that are virtually impossible to use in charted designs, such as glass mirrors, feathers, bits of fur, large beads, and wired ribbons. You are not limited by the charted design or the flatness of the canvas beneath your needle—animals spring to life, food looks good enough to eat, and you can almost smell the flowers bursting off the fabric.

Of the various surface embroidery techniques, crewel is probably the most well known. The primary feature of crewel is the variety of stitches, primarily used to mimic natural features but occasionally to add interesting texture to a piece. There are probably hundreds of different crewel stitches, but most people use only a few, perhaps a dozen in total, for most of their work. If you've done any needlework beyond very basic cross-stitch or needlepoint you'll recognize some of them—backstitch, blanket stitch, stem stitch, satin stitch, split stitch, and French knots are all frequently used.

Less commonly you'll find stitches like long and short stitch, detached buttonhole, fly stitch, bullion knot, wheat sheaf, and herringbone. The stitches used in this chapter are detailed below—if you'd like to learn more about the various crewel stitches, check out the books listed at the end of the chapter in the Resources section.

Blackwork is actually easier than crewel, but is less known. It was very popular in the European renaissance and can be seen in different forms (including freeform, counted, and smocking) on clothing in paintings from that period. Blackwork is any kind of simple embroidery that uses a single color of thread, usually black. Recently, redwork quilts have become popular again, and these consist of line drawings embroidered in red floss, usually in stem stitch or another simple line stitch. The three most common stitches for blackwork are backstitch, stem stitch, and split stitch—the idea is to reproduce a line drawing on your fabric. Counted blackwork is another technique that uses black thread to create a design on fabric, but this chapter uses non-counted blackwork that follows a printed pattern rather than the weave of the fabric.

Ribbon embroidery is a natural offshoot of crewel work and uses many of the same stitches to achieve a three-dimensional effect with 4-mm and 7-mm silk ribbons. Narrower and wider ribbons are also used, but these two are the most common sizes. Most ribbon embroidery motifs are flowers since the color, texture, and width of the ribbon lends itself well to recreating the shapes of delicate flower petals.

Or Nue looks complicated, the technique seems simple, but the finished product is somewhere in between. Not technically difficult to do for most needleworkers, it requires an eye for shading, the ability to lay the gold threads evenly, and a lot of patience. Or Nue is French for "shaded gold," and this technique was developed in the Middle Ages to decorate religious vestments. The Japan gold threads are couched down with various colors of silk or cotton floss, and this creates a shimmering golden image with lifelike shading. A truly breathtaking example, the finest one to exist in my opinion, is found on the Vestments of the Order of the Golden Fleece and features the Virgin Mary. In keeping with the traditionally sacred nature of both this style of embroidery and the gold threads, the Or Nue project in this chapter is of Hathor, an ancient Egyptian goddess connected to the golden sun god Ra.

The most complex form of surface embroidery bears the curious name of stumpwork; it was known prior to Victorian times as raised work. This highly three-dimensional form evolved primarily in the seventeenth century, although some raised work was known in Europe prior to that. Stumpwork, which probably gets its name from a type of shaded drawing popular at the time, involves the lavish use of wired forms, beads, feathers, and so on to create realistic plants, insects and other subject matter. Flowers literally pop off the fabric's surface in the form of wired shapes covered with stitching—insects shimmer with iridescent bead eyes; animals and people are stuffed with batting to give them the illusion of life. The stitches themselves are not difficult to master, but they need to be executed cleanly, and some embellishments use materials not usually found in embroidery, like large wooden beads that need to be covered evenly with threads. In addition, the meticulous finesse of creating and putting together the finished elements can be tedious because of the unfamiliar techniques, such as attaching wired forms and items like feathers to the base fabric. The results, however, are well worth any new tricks that must be learned and frustrations that must be overcome. The stumpwork project in this book is limited to wired leaves, a few different crewel stitches, and two seed beads—nothing an experienced stitcher can't handle with a bit of patience.

Speaking of patience, some of the projects here might seem overwhelming, or too difficult, but I have confidence in you! If you work the design in sections, you'll soon discover the project is springing to life under your needle and it won't seem so daunting. Take, for example, the Crewel Herb Neckline. All together, it seems to be a complicated design with many different plants and unfamiliar fibers to tackle. But wait . . . the yarrow is just split stitch and French knots. The sweetgrass is good old cotton floss done in satin stitches—easy! The velour fiber passes through the large hole made by the tapestry needle, and because of the fiber's size the sage and lavender leaves are done before you know it. Don't look at an overall design and get spooked—look instead at the individual parts that make up that design, and chances are you'll have no trouble working on it a little at a time.

Surface embroidery may be something less familiar to people than charted embroidery, but as mentioned earlier, it also means more freedom when it comes to materials. Traditional wool, cotton, and silk threads are joined by fantasy synthetics, and new finishing techniques that can make fibers shimmery, matte, nubby, or even covered with fuzzy "eyelashes." Hand-dyed fibers are all the rage, giving new dimensions of color to everything from silk ribbons to metallic blending filaments.

With this recent explosion of new materials for the needleworker, how does one choose what to use for an individual project? The simple answer is to let the project choose for you. Using the Crewel Herb Neckline as an example again, I wanted to simulate the natural textures of the plants as closely as possible. I picked a few sprigs of each plant and closely examined them so I could see how the light bounced off them. The velour made a perfect choice for the gentle downy leaves of the white sage and lavender, but I could have used matte cotton, wool, or suede leather strips, too. If you choose to wander off the list of fibers I've recommended for each project, feel free to experiment and see what works for you. Are you allergic to wool? Use matte cotton or a wooly synthetic. Don't like synthetics? Use perle cotton or Soie Platte silk for rayon-like shine instead. But whatever you do, be sure to send me a photo!

One thing that should be mentioned again, especially in a chapter discussing hand-dyed and unusual materials, is colorfastness. See the previous chapter, "Charted Needlework" for tips on how to check for color bleeding and how to care for your finished work.

Many techniques and materials are available to today's stitcher for transferring the designs to your fabric. On light-colored fabrics, I usually use sewing graphite or carbon paper between the original and the fabric (graphite washes out more readily than the carbon paper lines). The fabric needs to be secured to cardboard or otherwise immobilized so that the lines are accurate, else they can show outside the stitched areas.

Another technique is to hold the fabric over the original illustration and place them on a lightbox or in a bright window, then trace the design with a pencil. A disappearing or washable pen is another popular method—just be sure the fibers you're using won't bleed so that you can wash away the pen lines. Pouncing is a very old method, dating to medieval times, that involves pricking a series of holes in your design and then brushing chalk or graphite powder through them onto the fabric (I use this to apply quilting lines on my quilts).

You can also try freehanding the design or partially freehanding it. For the Stumpwork Lord of the Woods design, I laid the vellum pattern on top of the fabric and used a sewing pencil to draw the lines between the vellum and fabric. This way I could see where the tip of the pencil was as I drew—to try this method, copy the pattern onto vellum or tracing paper and use a sharp, light-colored sewing pencil (easily erased, they are usually available in white or pink). Before starting, you should do a test to see which method works best for you and your fibers.

Finally, all the projects assume the use of an embroidery hoop or other frame to hold the fabric taut. This prevents it from distorting and puckering as you put tension on it via the stitches. Some people like stitching without one, but I don't recommend it except perhaps for the Pomegranate and Pentacle Blackwork Border if it's done on a sleeve cuff, and on the Shisha Mirror Altar Cloth you may be able to get away with it if you usually stitch without a hoop and use very gentle tension.

The difficulty level of all these projects varies depending on your experience, preferred techniques, familiarity with the various stitches, and patience.

SHISHA MIRROR ALTAR CLOTH

"Shisha" is Hindi for "little glass" or "mirror," and these are often sewn onto clothing, bags, and other articles for a wonderful sparkle. These circular mirrors are cleverly stitched onto the edges of a plain cloth using copper braid to form an interwoven pentacle motif.

YOU'LL NEED:

Small prefinished altar cloth
Erasable colored sewing pencil
1-inch round mirrors (amount needed depends on cloth size)
Kreinik ⅛-inch copper braid
Scissors
#5 embroidery needle (or your choice)

Mark where each mirror will go around the edges of your altar cloth with the sewing pencil (remember to allow for the size of each mirror and any space between them). Lay a mirror on top of this mark and mark five small dots at equal points around the edge of the mirror. Make your first stitch with the braid from one dot to another dot on the opposite side, then move to the next dot over (on the back of the fabric) and come up for your next stitch. Continuing to form a pentagram shape, stitch this span of braid down and move to the next dot, coming up once again. At this point you'll need to start weaving the strands as necessary to form the over-under interwoven design of the pentagram. Do not pull your strands too tight or the fabric will pucker and distort—keep it stretched on a frame or laying flat on a table. Continue stitching until the five strands form a pentagram. Repeat for the remainder of the altar cloth border.

POMEGRANATE AND PENTACLE
BLACKWORK BORDER

Many people consider blackwork to be a geometric-charted form of needle-work, but freeform embroidery in black is also called blackwork (or redwork if done with red thread). Only one stitch is used—stem stitch—but the fine-ness and delicacy of this pattern makes it a challenge. Use tiny stitches and fine linen for best results. (Model stitched by Abigail Weiner.)

YOU'LL NEED:

    Fine linen article, such as a handkerchief or blouse
    Sewing carbon paper or washable fabric pen
    DMC cotton floss: 001 black
    Scissors
    Fine embroidery or quilting needle

Transfer the design to the fabric with sewing carbon paper or trace it using a washable fabric pen. Overlap the design so that it repeats to make it the desired length. Using one strand of floss, carefully follow all lines using very small stem stitches. Try to avoid leaving large knots or threads on the back that may show through the linen fabric by weaving in the ends.

The Crafty Witch

CREWEL HERB NECKLINE

This design is filled with medicinal and magical herbs—perfect for an herbalist or kitchen witch. A combination of European and Native American plants makes for an interesting variety of colors and textures, as does the unusual variety of fibers used to stitch them. Have fun stitching with wool, floss, matte cotton, and velour as the herbs come to life under your needle. (Model stitched by Karen Frank.)

YOU'LL NEED:

DMC Medicis wool: blanc, ecru, 8328, 8369, 8413
DMC cotton floss: blanc, 341, 434, 471, 612, 738, 3012, 3046, 3345, 3346
Needle Necessities Madras: 602
Needle Necessities Velour 18: 702, 706
Scissors
#5 or 6 embroidery needle
#22 or 24 tapestry needle
Laying tool (optional)
Shirt, blouse, dress, or robe

Enlarge the pattern to fit the neckline of your garment. If you'll be using it with an open-neck top, you can widen the pattern a bit by pivoting the two halves at the point of the star anise in the back. To do this, make another copy of the pattern and cut out the star anise. Cut the pattern in half between the rosemary and sweetgrass where there's a small gap, open it up as needed, transfer the design to the garment without the star anise, then lay the other copy of the star anise in the proper position to cover the union of the sage and white sage sprigs and transfer to the garment to complete the design.

Follow the stitching direction arrows when working each leaf. All flower blossoms (lavender, rosemary, yarrow) are done in French knots. Remember, there's no right or wrong way to stitch this design—if you don't like French knots, use another technique to fill in the flowers. If you prefer other materials or can't find the ones listed here, feel free to substitute as long as you maintain the basic texture and sheen of the leaves (you wouldn't want to use perle cotton for the white sage leaves, for example, but wool would work fine). Make the design your own!

HERB STITCH KEY:

Satin Stitch

French Knot

Split Stitch

Star Anise: floss (434, 738). With an embroidery needle, use satin stitch to work the basic star shape with 434 (3 strands), then go over each "petal" with a detached chain stitch in 738 (1 strand).

White Sage: velour (702, 706). With a tapestry needle and one strand of velour, work the larger leaves and outside edges of the smaller leaves with 702 in satin stitch, making a large hole for the fragile fiber to pass through or couching it instead. Work the inner portions of the smaller leaves with 706. If you have trouble with the velour coming apart, simply couch it in place with one strand of matching floss.

Mistletoe: madras (602). With an embroidery needle and three strands, satin stitch each leaf. This section looks especially good if you use a laying tool to lay the fibers flat on the top of the fabric as you work.

Yarrow: wool (blanc, ecru, 8328, 8413). Using an embroidery needle and two strands, work the yarrow leaves in split stitch with 8413. Using a random combination of blanc, ecru, and 8328, work the flower heads with French knots, sprinkling the colors in the area randomly.

Bay: floss (3346). With an embroidery needle and three strands, satin stitch the leaves. This area also looks especially good when the fibers are laid flat with a laying tool.

Rosemary: floss (blanc, 341, 3345). Thread two strands of blanc and two strands of 3345 in an embroidery needle and satin stitch the leaves. Randomly dot French knots in either blanc or 341 to create the rosemary flowers.

Sage: wool (8369). With an embroidery needle and one strand of wool, split stitch the leaves.

Lavender: velour (702, 706) and floss (341). With a tapestry needle and one strand of velour, satin stitch the leaves using 706 for the smaller leaves at the tips and 702 for the larger leaves farther

The Crafty Witch

down the stem, making a large hole for the fragile fiber to pass through or couching it instead. Use 706 for the flower stems. Using an embroidery needle and four strands of 341, create the flowers with French knots.

Sweetgrass: floss (471, 612, 3012, 3046). With an embroidery needle, satin stitch the grass using six strands where the braid is thicker and four strands at the thinner tip. Use the four colors as random stripes in each section to simulate the different colors of grass braided together. In the smaller sections where the braid gets tiny, use just one or two colors.

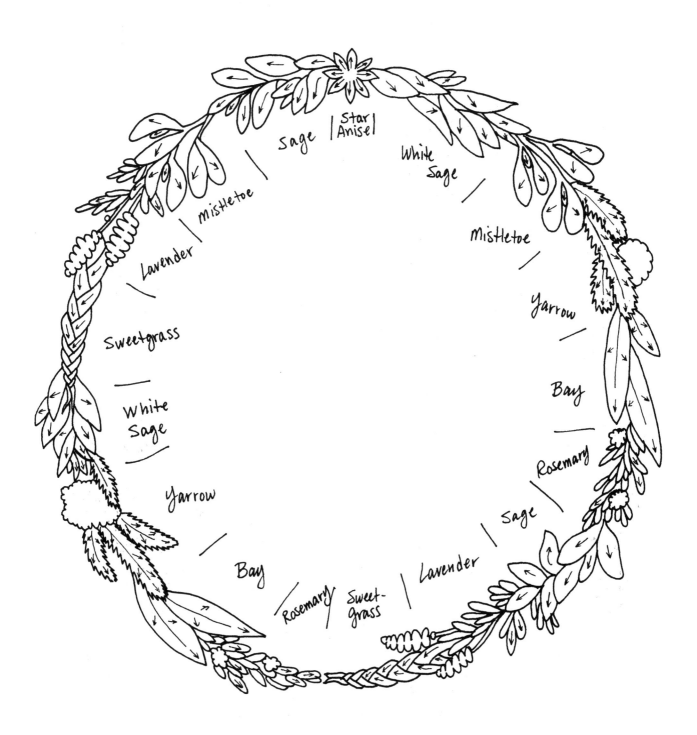

This well-known image by Mexican artist Jose Guadalupe Posada shows "Catrina," or "a well-dressed lady" in her brightly colored finery. Day of the Dead skeleton images like this one thumb their nose at death while still acknowledging that we all pass to the other side—many *offrendas* (ancestor altars) have funny skeleton scenes doing everything imaginable as well as colorfully decorated sugar skulls to remember those who have died. (Model stitched by Kim Mattox.)

YOU'LL NEED:

Black or other very dark color fabric
Light-colored fabric pencil
½-inch or ¾-inch lace with ribbon backing, your choice of color
    (I used pink)
Sewing thread or embroidery floss to match lace
Sewing needle
Scissors
DMC floss: blanc, 310, 444, 666, 3072
#3 and #6 embroidery needles
YLI Hand Dyed Silk Ribbon, 4-mm, colors 001 and 005
YLI Silk Ribbon, 4-mm, colors 029, 058, and 096
Elegance Ribbon to Dye For, 4-mm, color 3/4/13

Transfer the pattern to your fabric using a light-color fabric pencil. As always, work back to front, doing the items that appear farthest back in the design first and building from there. Start with the lace trim on the back

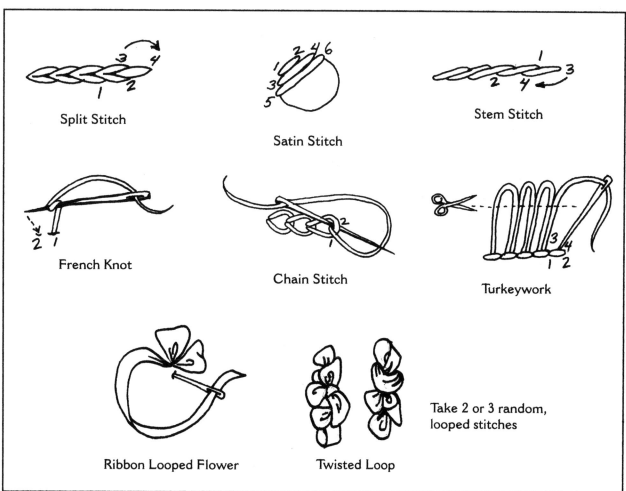

Split Stitch

Satin Stitch

Stem Stitch

French Knot

Chain Stitch

Turkeywork

Ribbon Looped Flower

Twisted Loop

Take 2 or 3 random, looped stitches

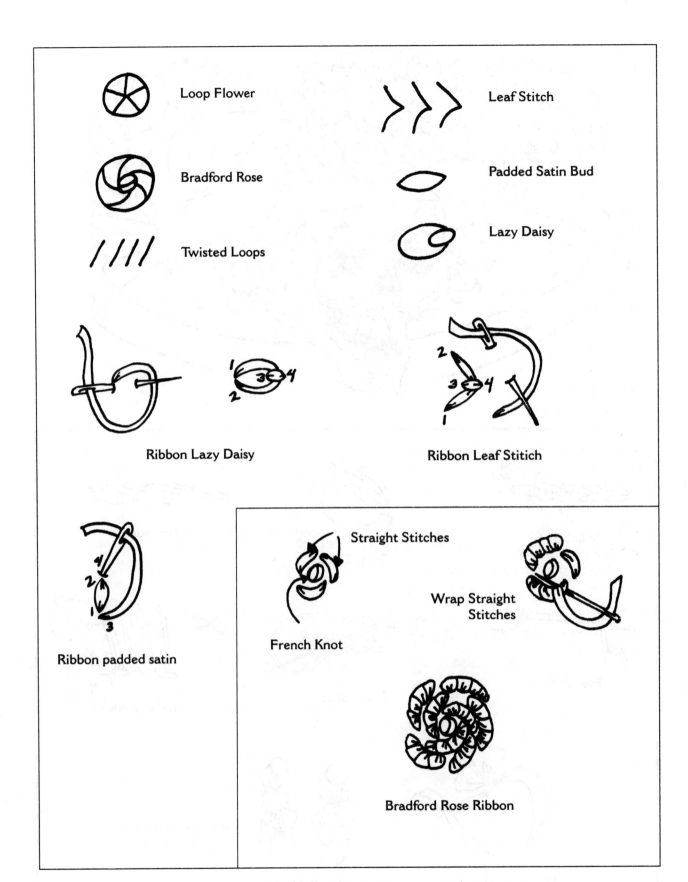

Loop Flower

Bradford Rose

Twisted Loops

Leaf Stitch

Padded Satin Bud

Lazy Daisy

Ribbon Lazy Daisy

Ribbon Leaf Stitich

Ribbon padded satin

Straight Stitches

French Knot

Wrap Straight Stitches

Bradford Rose Ribbon

Ribbon Catrina Key

half of the hat, folding down the top of the lace to hide the edge and folding under the ends at an angle to match the pattern. Stitch down the lace, adjusting it to match the curve of the shape and placing it over the jaw of Catrina's skull.

Using the smaller needle, stitch the underside of the hat with 3 strands of 310 black floss using split stitch. Stitch the skull with 2 strands of blanc, 310, and 3072 floss using split stitch as shown on the pattern and in the photograph. You will be stitching right over the lace put down in the previous step, so you may need to retrace the lower portion of the skull pattern onto the lace. Follow the directional lines in the shaded areas of the skull (color 3072). For the eyebrows and temple line, split stitch with 310. For finer lines such as around the teeth, stem stitch with 310 after the white sections are done. Satin stitch the tassels with 444 and 666 using 3 strands—either use 666 in the centers and 444 on the ends, or arrange the colors any way you like.

Add the second piece of lace on the front edge of the hat as shown on the pattern. You can fold down the top edge as before or leave the lace frilly on the top edge as desired. Split stitch the left edge of the hat with 310 as shown on the pattern by the black field.

Begin working on the silk ribbon hat embellishments by addressing the feather plumes first. For a fuller look fill in the feather areas with the grey floss using a 3-strand split or chain stitch (optional). Use a closely worked leaf stitch with medium grey (029) for the undersides of the plumes, then work the tops of the plumes with light grey (058). Next, work the lazy daisy stitches at the top of the hat using a random mixture of the yellow (005) and red (001) ribbon.

Stitch the four leaves with bright green (096) in padded satin stitch. There are two Bradford roses on the hat—work the smaller upper one with yellow (005) and the larger lower rose with red (001). Finish the hat by stitching the looped flowers with the pink and orange Elegance Ribbon (color 3/4/13).

In honor of this Egyptian goddess of love and beauty, I've chosen one of the most precious and exquisite needlework methods on earth to depict her. The gold cord evokes the treasures of ancient Egypt, and also reminds us that she is one of the "Eyes of Ra" and his daughter.

YOU'LL NEED:

2 pieces cotton muslin, approx. 8-inch × 12-inch
2 hanks Kreinik #5 Japan gold
DMC floss:

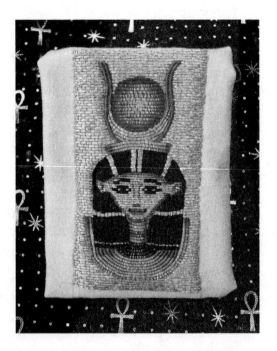

    310—black
    336—navy
    606—bright orange-red
    700—Christmas green bright
    702—kelly green
    780—topaz ultra very dark
    782—topaz medium
    783—Christmas gold
    797—royal blue
    817—coral red very dark
    3844—bright turquoise dark
    3845—bright turquoise medium
#8 embroidery needles (at least 3)
#20 blunt tapestry needle
Scissors

Stitch the muslin together to form two layers, stitching a 4-inch × 6-inch rectangle. This provides a sturdy, stable background fabric for the heavy metal threads that's still easy to stitch through. Transfer the design to the fabric in the center of this stitched area.

Work back to front, beginning with the background. Cut a 12-inch piece of Japan gold—any longer and the gold wrapping will begin to separate from the base fiber as it passes through the fabric repeatedly. Double the Japan gold in the tapestry needle (you will be couching down two strands at once), then come up in one corner of the design, wiggling the needle a bit to open a hole in the fabric to allow the gold to pass through more easily. Leave a loop on the back side that will be secured as you work the front. Stitch down the two paired gold strands with one strand of 783 every ⅛ inch or so. Near the end of the row, plunge the gold back down through the fabric as before. To begin the next row, come back up very close to the previous row and couch down as before with one strand of 783, but alternate these stitches every row so that the couching stitches form a brickwork effect.

In some areas you will need to satin stitch with the gold rather than coming up next to where you just went down. This is because the gold threads are stiff and will not lay flat, especially near the end of each row. In long rows you can couch the gold down and eliminate this problem, but in short rows the metal threads will form a gap and look uneven. Another tip to help reduce these gaps is to leave a short loop on the back when beginning a new row.

When the background is completed, move to the next layer, which is the colorful collar. Begin at the shoulder with the outermost row, which is scarlet. As before, lay the gold threads in pairs and use one strand of floss to couch it, curving the gold threads to match the shape of the collar as shown. At the shoulder of the collar and next to the hair, make several stitches in the darker color, then couch the rest of that collar row in the lighter color. For example, in the green rows, use 700 for several stitches, then change to 702. This gives a bit of shadow and depth to the collar, as if the hair is resting on top of it or the shoulder is curving away from you. Feel free to have two or three needles threaded at once as you work so that you don't have to keep rethreading them with the various colors. As you work toward the center of the collar, make larger gaps between the colored couching stitches so that the gold shows the most in the center and gives the illusion of being three dimensional.

The next two sections are the horns and black hair, and either of these can be worked first, as there is no overlap. The tips of the horns are worked closely in 780, especially on the outer edges so that they can be seen against the gold background. The inner sections of the horns and their base move from 782 to 783, spacing the stitches farther apart in the center as you did for the collar, to show depth and form.

When the horns are completed, stitch the scarlet solar disk horizontally using the two shades of floss to show depth. A few stitches at the top of the round disk are worked over *one* gold thread in order to give a smoother outline (look closely at the color photo for this detail). The hair is worked solidly with black, except for the gold wrappings which are formed by gaps in the black floss.

The face is stitched horizontally last over *one* strand of Japan gold. Use 780 at the edges and to form the ears and nose as shown. Use 310 for the eyes and 780 for the mouth. Stitch the bulk of the face with 783 in a loose brickwork pattern to allow the gold to show through.

STUMPWORK LORD OF THE WOODS

This creation is inspired by several deities, including Cernunnos, Pan, Sylvanus, and the Green Man. The spirit of wild nature, both the green plant and the stag, literally leaps forth from the fabric in this intricate raised embroidery piece that will be the source of pride and compliments for many years to come.

YOU'LL NEED:

    Dark monochromatic brown print cotton fabric
    Light-colored fabric pencil
    Large hoop or frame

The Crafty Witch

Scraps of unbleached quilting muslin

Embroidery hoop, approx. 6-inch diameter

Regular #2 pencil

Needle Necessities (NN) hand-dyed cotton floss:

- 120—antique parchment
- 121—saintly sins
- 128—serengeti
- 130—woodland fantasy
- 132—green with envy
- 133—British green

DMC cotton floss:

- White
- 310—black
- 904—parrot green very dark
- 906—parrot green medium

2 black seed beads

#12 beading needle or a small "sharp" to fit through the black beads

Scissors

Embroidery scissors with very fine tips, such as Gingher

32-gauge covered florist wire, both white and green

#5 or #8 embroidery needles (your preference)

#18 or #20 blunt tapestry needle

Round-nose jewelry pliers (optional)

Rubber needle grabber (optional)

For All Slips: Trace the pattern onto muslin with the pencil, then mount the fabric tightly in your hoop. Lay one end of the florist's wire at the beginning of each shape, leaving about an inch of wire free as a tail to secure the slip with later. Couch down the wire with 2 strands of the floss indicated, using round-nose jewelry pliers or your needle to help make sharp bends in the wire as you follow the outline. Trim any remaining wire to leave a 1-inch tail. Fill in the slip with close rows of split stitch using 3 strands of the same floss. Follow the direction arrows on the pattern when working the split stitch. When the slip is done, cut it out and trim away all muslin fabric with the fine-tip scissors, cutting extremely close to the wire edge so that no muslin is visible. To secure a slip, align it according to the Master Chart first, then use the tapestry needle to open holes for the wires to pass through to the underside. Once on the back, bend these wires back onto themselves and couch them down underneath the slip so the stitching doesn't show. Tack down the leaves in a few places as needed so that they stay in position, and bend the wire to make a wavy edge if you like (leaves only).

Master Pattern

Begin by tracing Pattern 1 onto the center of your brown fabric with the light fabric pencil. Refer to the Master Pattern and fill in the green background areas indicated with NN #133. Use 6 strands of floss and chain stitch. Fill in the antler tips with NN #121 using three strands and split stitch.

Pattern 1

Pattern 2: Work the eyes as padded satin stitch with DMC floss, following the stitch directions shown on the pattern and using 904 for the upper half of each iris and 906 for the lower half. Outline the eyes in split stitch with 2 strands of 310, making a double row for the thicker upper eyelashes. Use 1 strand of 310 to secure a black seed bead in the center of each eye. Also stitch the nostrils with a few satin stitches in 310. With NN #128, work the bottom half of each ear as split stitch using three strands. With a mixture of 2 strands NN #128 and 1 strand NN #121, stitch the upper half of each ear in turkeywork, trimming it so that it appears fur-like.

Use NN #130 for the mustache slip, NN #132 for the goatee slip, and NN #120 for the antler slips. The antlers are the most difficult slips to make and place, so take your time and work carefully. Note that there is a small break (about ⅛ inch wide) at the point where the antler passes under itself—

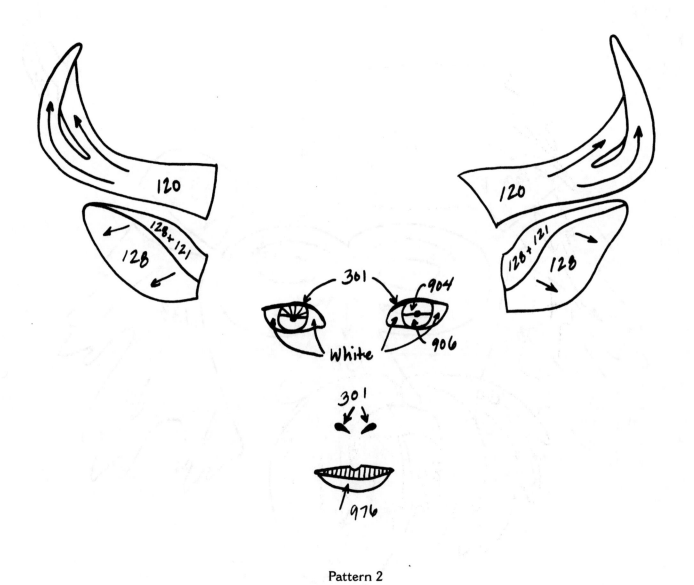

Pattern 2

The Crafty Witch

when you cut out these slips, you don't need to trim as close to this break since you will be covering the muslin with more stitching. Position and secure the three leaf-shaped slips, then position the antler slips, matching up your previous stitching just under the top edge of the slip. Plunge the wires underneath as you did with the previous slips, securing them on the back. Tack down the bottoms of the antler slips but do not tack down the tips. Instead, use NN #121 to continue the split stitching from the slips into the previously stitched antlers on the brown fabric so they match up and are relatively seamless. Bend the wired tip of the antler so that it floats just above this joined stitching area.

Pattern 3: Work the lips with 3 strands of a reddish-brown section of NN #128 in padded satin stitch. Use 6 strands of NN #130 to work the hair in split stitch, stitching right over the ends of the antlers and ears as shown.

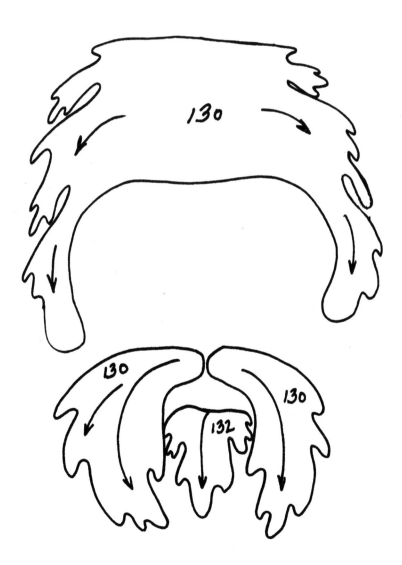

Pattern 3

Pattern 4: Make the three wired leaf slips for the face and stitch in place as shown.

Pattern 5: Make the two nose and eyebrow slips, then stitch in place as shown.

Pattern 4

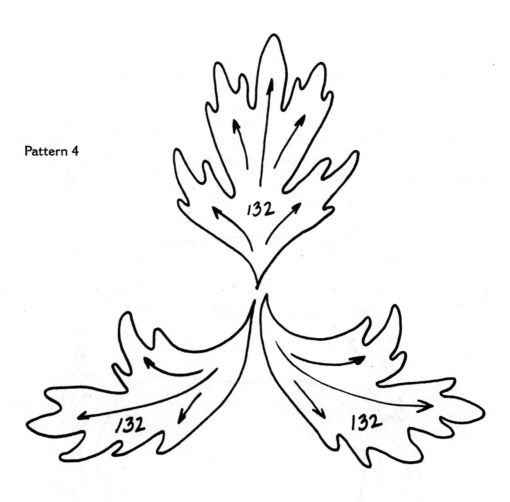

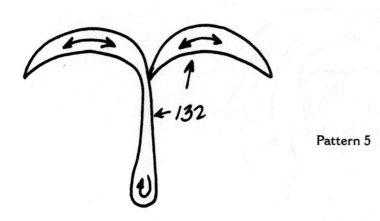

Pattern 5

The Crafty Witch

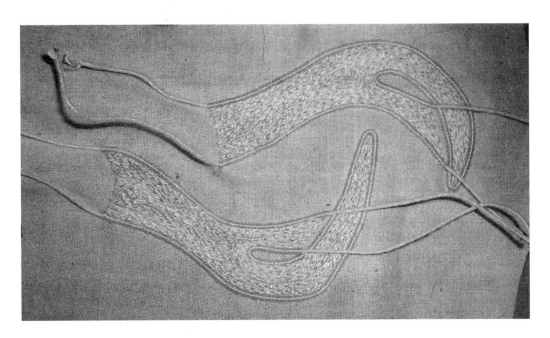

Antler slips

RESOURCES

The Cottage Discount Needlework
P.O. Box 864691
Plano, TX 75023
(888) 227-9988; www.discountneedlework.com

One of the few places to get silk ribbon for embroidery, and a great general resource.

Darice Inc.
13000 Darice Parkway, Park 82
Strongsville, OH 44149
(866) 432-7423; www.darice.com

A major manufacturer and distributor of craft supplies, Darice offers beads, round mirrors, and other interesting materials for the adventurous stitcher.

Kreinik Mfg. Co., Inc.
3106 Lord Baltimore Drive, Suite 101
Baltimore, MD 21244
(800) 537-2166; www.kreinik.com

Kreinik is the top supplier of metallic fibers for all kinds of needlework. Whether you need extra-fine metallic blending fibers, high-quality Japan threads, or shimmery variegated stitching braids, choose Kreinik.

Needle Necessities
7211 Garden Grove Boulevard, #BC
Garden Grove, CA 92841
(800) 542-7300; www.needlenecessities.com

This friendly family business specializes in creating high-quality hand-dyed needlework fibers. Sometimes subtle, sometimes spectacular, the variety of colors and fibers available here will keep you busy for a long time. Quickly becoming one of my very favorite embroidery fiber suppliers.

Nordic Needle, Inc.
1314 Gateway Drive SW
Fargo, ND 58103
(800) 433-4321; www.nordicneedle.com

Just about any kind of needlework fiber and book you could possibly want! An amazing selection of materials for the serious stitcher.

The Quilters' Resource, Inc.
P.O. Box 148850
Chicago, IL 60614
(800) 676-6543; www.quiltersresource.com

This is a wholesale company, but on their website you can explore their hand-dyed silk ribbons such as the one used in the Catrina project in this chapter.

3

*Y*arn

Okay, you win. . . . I heard the (numerous!) complaints that there were no yarn crafts in the previous book, so I made sure to include this chapter to get myself out of trouble! Now, I don't want to hear complaints about the lack of knitting projects because (1) I really don't like to knit and I'm not very good at it, (2) a recent survey of crafters showed that two-thirds preferred crochet over knitting, and (3) the field is wide open for another lovely Pagan crafter to write her own book filled with knitting projects. Ha.

Having covered all my bases (I hope!), let's move on to the materials and techniques used in this chapter. First, the battle between natural versus synthetic deserves a little time. This was a hot topic recently on an Internet craft list I was on, and for good reason. Which is more earth-friendly? Which is more practical to use? What does "synthetic" or "natural" mean anyway?

Let's look at a skein of yarn. A lot of yarn these days is synthetic, meaning that it's spun out of some form of plastic, which is derived from petroleum products. Some will argue that petroleum comes from the earth, as does everything else (unless it comes from outer space), and thus everything is "natural." But the manufacture of these fibers, from drilling for the oil to spinning the strands, releases toxic chemicals into the environment. It's also non-biodegradable, which means that if someone digs up your trash in 2,000 years, your doll-shaped toilet paper cover will still be as good as the day Grandma made it for you.

The rest of the yarn on the shelf is probably cotton or wool. Cotton, unless it's organically grown, is one of the top users of pesticides, an average of nearly 6 pounds per acre. And unless you're sure of how the animals are treated, wool wanders into the nasty realm of animal cruelty on factory farms. If you're lucky enough to be able to afford silk, the worms are boiled alive in their cocoons to retrieve the fiber. So what's a crafter to do?

If you're not interested in spinning your own wool (as I do on occasion), there's a whole new generation of organic and recycled fibers available in catalogs and specialty shops. Recycled clothing and pop bottles, cruelty-free raw or wild silk and soy protein fibers are all being made into gourmet yarns for the new generation crafter. If you can't afford these upscale fibers, try checking thrift stores and yard sales for these and other yarns. In my personal opinion, I weigh the good with the bad of producing each fiber and generally choose cotton when I can, if for no other reason than it's the most biodegradable. But you're certainly welcome to use whatever yarn you like, as long as it's the same size and weight so the finished project works out the same.

The projects in this book use either #10 crochet thread (also called bedspread weight), sport weight, or worsted weight. If these terms are mysterious, don't worry—the skein will tell you the yarn's size. For the crochet projects, I've used both a Tunesian hook and various standard hooks. There appears to be two different hook styles, one wide and one narrow. If you're a beginner I recommend the narrower hook made by Boye as it's less likely to snag adjacent yarn and will slide through the loop more easily, but again, this is a purely personal preference.

If you've never done crochet in your life, you probably should learn how before trying these projects. Crochet is really very easy once you know how, and it's based on just a few simple stitches that all involve pulling a loop of yarn through another loop. There are many books, magazines, and websites available that show basic crochet techniques and stitches if you need a little extra help beyond the scope of this book.

Two of the projects don't involve crochet at all, and if you're just starting out or are working with children, these may be the best to begin with. Twisting individual strands into a rope is extremely simple, and multiple strand finger weaving is very easy as well. Can you make a three-strand braid? You can finger weave!

Crochet Glossary: ch = chain; dc = double crochet; dec = decrease; inc = increase; sc = single crochet; st = stitch; sl st = slip stitch

TWISTED CORD CINGULUM

This is about as easy as working with yarn can get. If you want something more unusual than just a plain rope, try substituting "eyelash" or other specialty yarn of the same weight. When selecting your colors, remember that your twist will get doubled back on itself so you'll have twice the strands that you start out with when it's done. This is an ideal project for a group since it's far easier and turns out better with the help of another person.

YOU'LL NEED:

    1 skein of yarn in each of the colors you wish to use (any weight
        yarn, but medium weight such as sport or worsted is best)
    Scissors
    Coat hanger (optional)
    Hand mixer, electric screwdriver, or hand drill (optional)
    Large tapestry needle (optional)

Cut lengths of yarn approximately 20 feet in length to match the colors your group uses, or what is personally meaningful to you. Don't use more than about 6 strands of sport or 4 strands of worsted, or the finished cord will be too thick (3 strands of worsted gives the cord pictured, which is about a half inch thick).

Tie the strands together at one end in a simple knot and either have a friend help you or secure it to something like a sewing machine thread spindle or the top of a coat hanger so that it can be slipped off easily when you're done twisting. Hold the other end of the yarn strands and begin twisting them in one direction. You can also place a single beater in your hand mixer and tie the strands to this to twist it more quickly (or attach it to a screwdriver or drill).

Continue twisting the strands until a very tight rope is formed and it's naturally inclined to twist back on itself. Hold the very center of the rope and fold it in half so that the two ends meet (this is where having a friend help is best). Carefully and gently help the rope twist back on itself to form a double-thickness rope. When it stabilizes itself, tie a knot in each end about two inches from the end and trim to make fringe. Alternately, you can measure exactly how long you want the cord to be and tie the knots there. If desired, you can use a large needle to tease apart the ends of the fringe so that it's more delicate and wavy.

FINGER WOVEN CINGULUM

Finger weaving is just as easy as braiding, there's just more of it. The project pictured was made as part of a ritual that involved each of the planets in our solar system. Your cingulum can have as many strands as you like and each one can have a special meaning to you and/or your group.

YOU'LL NEED:

1 skein of yarn in each of the colors you wish to use (any weight yarn, but medium weight such as sport or worsted is best)
Scissors
Coat hanger (optional)
Large tapestry needle (optional)

Cut the yarn in approximately 12-foot lengths for a 9-foot cingulum. Tie all the strands together a few inches from one end and secure it to a sewing machine thread spindle or the top of a coat hanger so that it can be slipped off easily when you're done.

Lay the strands so that they are flat next to each other. Take the strand farthest on the left (or right, your choice) and lay it over the strand next to it. Weave the strand under the next, over the next, and so on until all the strands are integrated. The second strand will now be on the end, so pick that one up and do the same, weaving over and under until you reach the opposite side (this strand should alternate with the first, so that it goes over one the previous one went under, and so on).

Simply continue taking the strand on the end and weaving to continue the pattern. Occasionally you will need to untangle the other end as you work. When you reach the desired length, tie a knot in the work so that it doesn't unravel, then trim to size. If desired, you can tease out the fringe with a large needle to create a smaller, wavy fringe at the ends.

FILET CROCHET "MERRY MEET" FLAG

Filet crochet is perhaps one of the easiest forms of this craft because all it involves is chains and double crochet stitches, nothing fancy at all. This lacy project will welcome visitors with a pretty floral design that incorporates meaningful symbols and a heartfelt message. (Model crocheted by Kristal Wildman.)

YOU'LL NEED:

> 1 skein white or ivory worsted-weight yarn
> Crochet hook, size F
> Scissors
> Large blunt tapestry needle

When working filet crochet, there are solid blocks and empty blocks as seen on the graph. For solid over solid, simply crochet into the tops of the next 3 stitches as you would with normal crochet. For empty over solid, ch 2, skip next 2 dc, dc in next dc (see glossary on page 52 for abbreviations). For solid over empty, dc 2 in ch 2 space, dc in next dc. For empty over empty, ch 2, dc in next dc. The stitches bordering each block are shared by both blocks—each block has 4 total stitches if isolated, but the stitches on each end are shared by the adjacent block.

Begin at the top of the banner and ch 42. Dc in the 4th ch from the hook (the skipped ch count as your first dc). Follow the graph until row 57.

Row 57: sl st in next 3 dc, ch 3 to start the row (counts as first dc). Continue following the chart to the end of the row, ending one block early as shown on the chart for a total of 38 st in this row.

Continue using this decrease method to create the curved bottom of the banner until the end of the chart. Finish off and weave in the end of the yarn.

To hang the banner, make a very long chain with the same yarn (or use white cotton string) and string it through the staggered holes found in row 1. Use this yarn or string to hang it from the pole horizontally.

FILET CROCHET ALTAR CLOTH

Like the previous project, this creates a lacy design that's easy to make. But unlike the large flag, size 10 crochet thread is used instead. Try making it in either very light or very dark solid colors, perhaps in black laid over a silver cloth or in ivory over a dark green cloth.

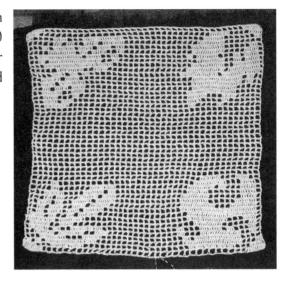

YOU'LL NEED:

   1 ball #10 crochet thread
   Steel crochet hook, size 6 (approx. 1.8 mm)
   Scissors
   Blunt tapestry needle

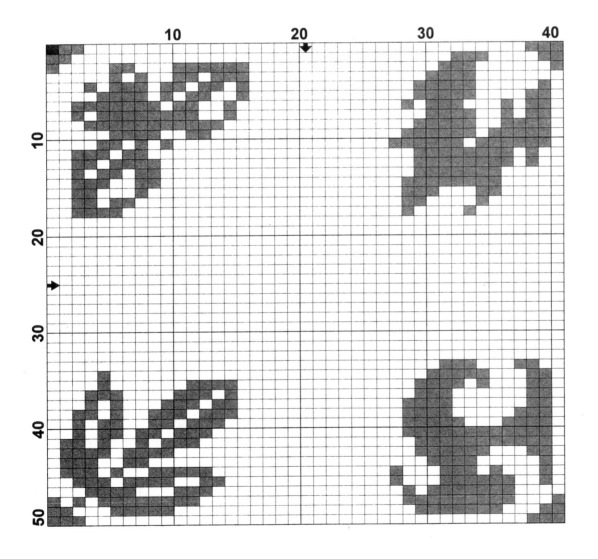

See the first paragraph of the previous project for a basic explanation of working filet crochet. Start at the "Earth/Air" end of the chart at the bottom and work your way up. Ch 154, then dc in the 4th ch from the hook (skipped ch count as first dc). Follow the chart as shown, finish off and weave in all ends.

CROCHET BEADED KERCHIEF

Here's a fun project that can be done in whimsical colors for a girl or dramatic colors for a midnight ritual. Experiment with colors and different shapes of beads for different looks.

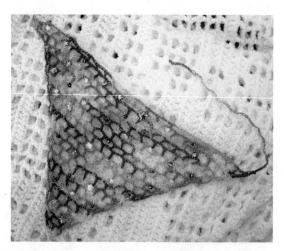

YOU'LL NEED:

1 ball variegated #10 crochet thread
  (your choice of color)
55 assorted star-shaped beads between
  6 mm and 12 mm
Crochet hook, size E
Tapestry needle
Scissors
Blunt tapestry needle

Begin by threading all the beads onto the crochet thread.

Row 1: ch 8, join in 1st ch with sl st.

Row 2: ch 4, dc in 6th ch of row 1, ch 2, dc in 4th ch of row 1, ch 5, turn.

Row 3: dc in 1st space, ch 1, ch bead, ch 1, dc in 2nd space, ch 2, dc in 2nd space, ch 5, turn.

Row 4: dc in 1st sp, ch 3, dc in top of ch bead, ch 3, dc in space, ch 3, dc in space again, ch 5, turn (4 spaces total).

Row 5: dc in 1st space, ch 1, ch bead, ch 1, dc in space, ch 3, dc in space, ch 1, ch bead, ch 1, dc in space, ch 3, dc in space again, ch 5, turn.

Continue in this pattern, alternating rows of ch bead with rows of spaces, until you are out of beads. Work one more row of spaces, then work about 9 inches of chain. Finish off. Join to the beginning of this same row and work another 9 inches of chain (these are the ties for the kerchief—adjust their length to fit the wearer). Finish off and weave in all ends.

TUNESIAN CROCHET WIZARD SCARF

When you get your Tunesian hook, it will come with basic instructions for how to work the knit stitch. This easy stitch is something like a variation on knitting using one needle. It sounds strange, but it can be really fun and addictive. Luckily, more and more patterns are becoming available for this unique crochet technique. The design will delight wizards and witches of all ages, and any color combination can be easily substituted if burgundy and gold don't suit your personality.

YOU'LL NEED:

2 skeins each: 2.5 oz Red Heart Sport yarn, 0918 vermillion, 0230 yellow (or substitute equivalent burgundy and golden yellow sport weight yarn)
Tunesian crochet hook, size L-11
Scissors
Ruler
Large blunt tapestry needle

Ch 31, work Tunesian knit stitch for 30 stitches across, 20 rows each color. Start with burgundy, then switch to golden yellow, alternating them for a total of 8 burgundy sections and 7 gold sections.

For the fringe: Cut 42 lengths of burgundy yarn 14 inches long, and 36 lengths of gold yarn 14 inches long. Divide the yarn into groups of 3 strands, and fold these in half. Tug on the very edge of the scarf end and you'll find that natural holes form between the rows of knit stitches. From the back, put the crochet hook through the natural hole at one of the corners. Pull 3 folded strands of the burgundy yarn through the hole and make a lark's head knot, pulling on the fringe so that it comes out even as you tighten the knot. Pull 3 more strands through the opposite corner. Working toward the center in every other hole, alternate gold and burgundy lark's head knots until the edge is filled up with fringe. You may need to fudge the position of the very center fringe to fit—you should have 7 burgundy knots and 6 gold knots total. Repeat for the other end of the scarf. Trim the fringe ends evenly if desired.

The fringe should help weight the ends down so they don't curl so much, but as Tunesian crochet naturally tends to curl a bit, you may need to occasionally block the scarf to keep it flatter.

TAPESTRY CROCHET DRAGON
TAROT BAG

Dr. Carol Ventura, whose help was invaluable for developing this project, has studied indigenous methods for this unusual crochet technique. If this project tickles your fancy, check out her books for more tapestry crochet patterns and ideas. The thicker, more stiff texture of this stitch lends itself well to more durable items, like bags, play balls, bowls, and rugs.

YOU'LL NEED:

1 ball each Lily Sugar 'n Cream cotton worsted yarn in dark pine and purple variegated
Crochet hook, size H
Safety pin or stitch marker
Scissors
Large blunt tapestry needle

Round 1: Using the purple yarn, leave a 3–4-inch tail, make a sl st and chain 21. Starting with the 2nd chain from the hook, sc to the end of the ch, working 2 sc in the last ch (22 st total). Continue to sc using the bottom of the original chain until you come around to the first stitch, carrying the yarn tail on top of the previous row as you go. The tail will end up in the middle of the sc stitches. Sc 2 st into the last st (42 st total). Because this is worked in a spiral manner, it's important to keep track of where the previous row ended, so slip a stitch marker into the last stitch before continuing.

Round 2: Cut the tail as necessary and begin carrying the green yarn. Sc around without increases, carrying the green yarn so that the round is the proper thickness. Turn the pouch right side out (the start of the pouch has been worked inside out). As you carry the yarn inside the stitches, you may need to gently tug on it so that it sits inside neatly, since it will occasionally become loose and bulge out from between the stitches unattractively.

Round 3: Continue carrying the yarn inside the stitches and sc for 4 st, then begin the charted dragon design. To switch colors, lay the current color on top of the previous row of stitches, then bring the new color out from behind and continue crocheting. Pull the threads gently as needed to maintain an even design and to keep the yarn colors concealed inside when not in use.

Continue until the dragon pattern is complete. Gently tug on the pouch to make it lay flat (the tips of the wings should appear to be about 1 stitch from the edge of the pouch side). Work 1 more row of only variegated purple, concealing the green in the center as usual. When the end of the row is reached, clip the green yarn and work 3 rows of regular double crochet. Finish off.

For the drawstring, braid or chain either color of yarn until it's as long as desired. Weave this drawstring in and out of the first row of dc and knot the ends together.

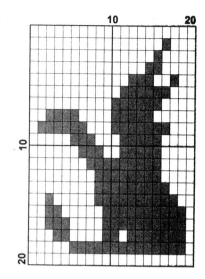

TAPESTRY CROCHET
SHAMAN'S BASKET

Based on the traditional willow and sedgeroot coiled baskets of the California Indians, this project with a different twist makes a soft yet secure place to stash your altar treasures. Shaman baskets were kept hidden within the belongs of the village healer or magicworker and contained sacred objects such as cocoon rattles, healing herbs, and special talismans. Very few survive because a person's belongings, especially their magic tools and baskets, were cremated with them when they died. Additionally, basket designs were not copied between the weavers, because it was believed that in doing so that a little of the weaver's power would be taken as well. This project, freely shared since it is not a traditional basket, is a special tribute to our Native American ancestors.

YOU'LL NEED:

> 1 ball each Lily Sugar 'n Cream cotton worsted yarn in cream (or tan, your choice), warm brown, and black
> G-hook (4.25 mm, slightly larger is fine too)
> Scissors
> Safety pin or crochet stitch marker
> Large blunt tapestry needle

This project is worked in spiral rounds, meaning that the basket coils up one row on top of the previous one rather than reversing at the end of a flat row. The entire project is worked in single chain (sc).

Round 1: Starting with cream (or tan), make a slip knot and chain 4. Slip stitch to join and make a ring. Work 6 sc stitches (st), carrying the tail end of the yarn in the center of the stitches. It should lay on top of the previous row as you work. Mark your place and at the beginning of each new row so you can find the first stitch when you come back around to it.

Round 2: Cut the tail and begin carrying black. Increase (inc) in every stitch so that you end up with 12 st.

Round 3: inc in every st (24 st).

Round 4: inc in every 2nd st (36 st).

Round 5: inc in every 3rd st (48 st).

Round 6: sc the entire round with no inc.

Round 7: inc in every 8th st (54 st).

Round 8: inc 1. Begin chevron pattern by switching to (1 black sc, 5 cream sc), 8 times. 1 black, 3 cream.

Round 9: Continue pattern with (3 black, 4 cream, 3 black, 3 cream), 4 times. 3 black, 3 cream, 3 black, inc with cream, 1 cream.

Round 10: Continue pattern with (5 black, 2 cream, 5 black, cream inc) 4 times. 6 black (63 st).

Round 11: 1 black (inc black, 1 black, 1 cream, 4 black) 8 times, 1 black, 1 cream, inc black, 2 black.

Round 12: 4 black (3 cream, 5 black) 8 times, 3 cream, 2 black.

Round 13: 2 black (5 cream, 3 black) 8 times, 5 cream, 1 black.

Round 14: 2 black 1 cream in same st as last black, 6 cream (1 black, 7 white) 8 times, 1 black.

Round 15: Begin carrying brown. 4 cream, decrease (dec) by skipping the next st, continue with cream dec every 7 stitches, 4 st to the end of the round. The last st. should now go into the black st of the previous row. This makes it easier to find your place. Adjust the end of your round as needed.

Round 16: dec in the first st (5 brown, 1 cream dec) 9 times (the 3rd brown st in the last repeat is in the previous row decrease).

Round 17: (1 cream, 3 brown, 1 cream dec) 8 times, 1 cream, 3 brown, 1 cream.

Round 18: 2 cream (2 brown, 1 cream, 1 cream dec) 9 times.

Round 20: 1 cream (1 brown, 3 cream) 8 times, 1 brown, 1 cream. Clip off brown, join in previous row with 1 cream slip st, end off, weave in end.

RESOURCES

Annie's Attic
306 East Parr Road
Berne, IN 46711
(800) 282-6643; www.anniesattic.com

A well-known mail-order catalog that offers more than just yarn, they have materials for all kinds of needlecrafts, too. A good basic resource with a variety of crochet and knitting supplies such as yarn and hooks. This is one of the only places to get the Tunesian crochet hooks and instructional materials.

Lily
320 Livingstone Avenue South
Listowel, Ontario, N4W 3H3, Canada
www.sugarncream.com

Lily is one of the best and most well-known manufacturers of cotton crochet yarns in the world. Their lead product, "Sugar 'n Cream" is a worsted-weight cotton yarn that is such a top seller that Wal-Mart has tried to copy it with their own brand, but don't be fooled—buy the original from Lily if you want real quality and color selection. Many colors of Sugar 'n Cream are also available in large cones for bigger projects.

Wrights
85 South Street, P.O. Box 398
West Warren, MA 01092
(877) 597-4448; www.wrights.com

Manufacturer of Boye crochet hooks in both larger aluminum and small-size steel. I prefer Boye hooks because their slim profile doesn't catch in your yarn as much as other brands I've tried. The aluminum hooks come in a variety of colors, so you can either collect a matched set, or choose a different color for each size so they're easy to identify. Available as individual hooks or graduated sets.

Yarndex
12936 Stonecreek Drive, Unit C
Pickerington, OH 43147
www.yarndex.com

A fantastic resource that enables you to find just about any yarn and fiber in the universe for your knitting and crochet projects. Yarndex isn't a store, but each fiber listing has a "where to buy" section so you can find the type of yarn you're looking for and then click over to another site to buy it.

4

Fabric

"The fabric of our lives" isn't just a catchphrase from the cotton industry, it truly is a metaphor we can all understand. Fabric can be a wedding gown or a funeral pall . . . it can be a commercial tote bag or the blanket swaddling a newborn baby. . . . It can be the robes of Tutankhamen or the Shroud of Turin. Fabric can be whatever we want or need it to be, no matter what your walk of life or era of time.

You can use fabric to express yourself in lots of creative ways. In this chapter, fabric forms a useful canvas tote bag for your ritual gear, groceries, or books. It serves as a backdrop for a humorous T-shirt, a quickly sewn altar cloth, a symbolic expression of freedom, and as a ritual costume accessory.

Many craft techniques are explored in this chapter, such as stamping, painting, sewing by machine, hand stitching, and embellishment with non-fabric supplies. There's no limit to what you can do with fabric as an artistic medium, and there are so many kinds of fabrics available to play with that it's hard to know where to begin.

The materials used to form the fabric and its resulting weave play a huge part in how the fabric will work for the project you have in mind. A heavy cotton canvas obviously isn't suitable for delicate costume wings, nor is a sheer synthetic appropriate for a traditional Egyptian nemyss, which was originally made from heavy stiffened linen. Also think ahead to how the project will be used when selecting your fabric. For example, if a shimmery synthetic could burst into flames if it gets near a candle, don't use it for your ritual robes!

How fabric is handled and laundered also depends on what it's made of and how it's made. A knitted wool sweater, when washed in a machine, will turn into a doll-size felted garment (desirable when making felted slippers or mittens on purpose), but most wool fabrics are machine washable with no ill effects. Some synthetics are so delicate you can't use an iron with them, whether you're trying to remove candle wax or apply iron-on embellishments to a costume piece. It pays to look at the fabric's care label when at the store before buying it or making the desired item.

Be realistic about your own sewing abilities and the capability of your sewing machine to handle what you're about to run through it. I know my beloved old 1893 treadle Singer will handle anything, even several layers of denim or canvas, but it's a real struggle to work with knits or slippery synthetics on it, especially since it has no zigzag stitch. It's also a good idea to make a practice mockup item out of inexpensive cotton muslin if you're not sure how it goes together, how your machine will handle the real fabric, or your ability to work with specialty fabrics.

This chapter begins with no-sew projects that involve only painted designs on pre-made items. As the difficulty level increases, we move into basic machine sewing with easy-to-use quilting cottons, then progress to a hand-sewn Penny Rug Candle Mat that uses wool felt fabric. Nothing here is too terribly difficult, especially if you have some experience with fabric, sewing, or fabric craft techniques and adhesives.

Fabric is very forgiving as well as easy to work with in general. And most kinds of fabric are inexpensive enough that you can spend just a couple of dollars to get a little extra as "goof insurance." So dive right in to the easy projects, and perhaps learn a new trick or two while making the harder ones at the end of the chapter.

STAMPED CANVAS TOTE BAG

Using a pre-made tote, two foam stamps, and just a few earthy colors, this project works up quickly and will gain a lot of compliments. Just a hint of gold shimmer at the tips of the leaves make it a little extra special, too.

You'll Need:

Pre-made canvas tote in natural/ivory
Piece of scrap cardboard
Delta craft paint: black, kelly green, golden yellow, metallic gold
Delta fabric medium
Paper plate
½-inch flat paint brush
Small container of water to rinse brush
Foam rubber stamps, large oak leaf and Celtic knot

Wash the tote according to the attached instructions to remove any fabric sizing (finishing chemicals from the factory) that might prevent the paint from adhering properly. Dry and iron flat. Place the cardboard inside so that the paint doesn't leak through the fabric and mark the inside or back of the bag.

Pour a small amount of black paint and green paint onto the paper plate and mix the fabric medium into each color according to the instructions on the bottle. Using the paint brush, dab small amounts of black onto the Celtic knot foam stamp in a random pattern, then dab green onto the stamp randomly, making a mottled black and green color throughout the knot design. Work quickly, since acrylic paint dries very fast. Stamp the tote bag in the bottom corner, then paint the stamp and repeat until you have 6 knot motifs on the bag.

Pour a small amount of golden yellow and metallic gold paint onto the paper plate and add fabric medium to each color. Using all 4 colors, paint the leaf stamp with the darkest color in the center and the golden yellow at the edge, with metallic gold at the very tips and overlapping the yellow. Stamp the leaf in a random way above the knot stamps, and repeat until this area contains as many leaves as desired, overlapping them if you like.

"CRANKY MOTHER" PAINTED SHIRT

If you have those PMS sorts of days and are over the age of about 40, you'll enjoy making and wearing this fun shirt that can be done on a tee or sweatshirt. It also makes a great gift for your favorite crone-to-be with a good sense of humor.

YOU'LL NEED:

    Blank T-shirt or sweatshirt in a pale color (white, ivory, mint green, pink, etc.)
    Piece of scrap cardboard to fit inside shirt
    Sewing carbon paper
    Fabric paints in brown, red, and black

Wash the shirt to remove any fabric sizing so the paint will adhere properly. Iron if necessary so the shirt is perfectly flat. Slide the cardboard inside so the paint doesn't mark the inside or back of the shirt. If the shirt is pale and/or thin enough, enlarge the pattern and tape it to the cardboard so

I'm not a CRONE

I'm just a cranky MOTHER

that you can trace it directly. Otherwise, either freehand the letters or use washable sewing carbon paper to copy the design onto the shirt (do not use typing carbon paper which will not wash out).

The word CRONE should be done in black, and the word MOTHER should be done in red. All other words are done in brown. Leave the cardboard in place and allow the paint to dry completely according to the instructions on the bottle.

SUPER SIMPLE ALTAR CLOTHS

A yard of novelty fabric, some scissors, a sewing machine, and in about 15 minutes you have a great altar cloth. These are about 36 inches square, and fit medium to large spaces—if your space is smaller (such as a narrow buffet or countertop), simply fold up the fabric to fit. The price is right, too—quilting cottons run less than $10 a yard, and I think that's a pretty good price for a machine washable, sturdy altar cloth.

YOU'LL NEED:

    1 yard of fabric
    Scissors
    Matching thread
    Sewing machine or needle

If using cotton or other fabric that may shrink, wash first and dry in a hot dryer. Cut the fabric so that it makes a neat square about 36 inches across in both directions. Fold the edges under ¼-inch, then under again to enclose the raw or selvage edge, and stitch. Clip threads.

SIMPLE EGYPTIAN NEMYSS

This traditional royal headdress is very quick and simple to make, easy to put on and take off, and works well in an Egyptian-theme ritual. You can get 2 from ⅔ of a yard of fabric, or 3 from a whole yard. It can be difficult to find just the right striped fabric—the stripes should be between ⅜-inch at the narrowest and ⅞-inch at the widest for the right proportion (½-inch is really optimal). You can also either dye a black and white stripe with gold dye for a kingly look, or use a variety of fabric colors to match the occasion or a deity's traditional color (green for Bast and Hathor, red for Set and Sekhmet, turquoise for Ptah and Thoth, and so on).

YOU'LL NEED:

⅔ to 1 yard of striped cotton or linen fabric

Scissors

Thread to match the darker stripe color

Sewing machine

Starch or iron to shape the finished nemyss (optional)

Enlarge the pattern so that it's 22 inches wide (at the front) by 20¾-inches long (running the direction of the stripes). You may need to piece the pattern together. Fold the fabric in half in the direction of the stripes so that the fabric is doubled under the pattern. Lay the pattern on top of the fabric, following the direction of the stripes, and cut carefully around it. For each nemyss, also cut 2 strips of fabric 12 inches × 2 inches (these are the ties which will be hidden and can be any color or stripe direction).

Hem the edges by folding under ¼ inch twice to enclose the raw edge, then stitch around the edges. Fold the ties so that the raw edges are inside, and stitch. In the front corners where indicated, on the underside of the fabric, stitch the ties to the nemyss by stitching a little square inside the edges of the ties to attach them very securely. If desired, you can add starch and/or iron the finished nemyss to make it stand out more stiffly in the familiar triangular fashion.

The Crafty Witch

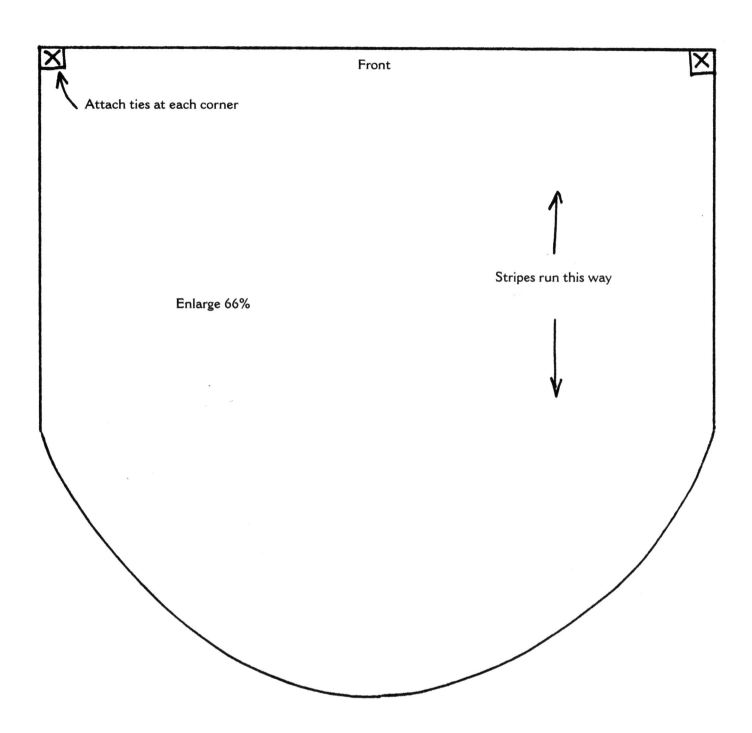

Front

Attach ties at each corner

Stripes run this way

Enlarge 66%

Simple Egyptian Nemyss

71

PIECED AMERICAN FLAG WITH
PENTACLE STARS

The basic flag is made exactly like a traditional American flag—your job is to add the stars to the blue field, which in this case happen to be magical white pentacles. It's okay if you can't fit all 50 stars in the blue field. . . in fact, you don't even have to try! Just have fun with the design and it'll turn out great.

You'll Need:

1 yard each of red and white fabric

½ yard of royal blue fabric

Iron

Scissors

Sewing machine (or needle if you want to be Betsy Ross)

Red thread

Scrap cardboard or several layers of newspaper

1-inch Pentacle rubber stamp

White or silver opaque stamp ink, such as Lumiere metallic silver or pearl white, neopaque white, or Textile Traditionals super opaque white

Dry stamp pad (optional, for bottled inks that don't come on a pre-inked pad)

All seams are ¼-inch wide. Wash and iron all fabric before starting. Cut the red fabric into 7, 2-inch-wide strips, 4 of them 11 inches long, 3 of them 26 inches long. Cut the white fabric into 6, 2-inch-wide strips, 3 of them 11 inches long, 3 of them 26 inches long. Cut the blue fabric into a rectangle measuring 11 inches × 15 inches. Stitch together the 7, 11-inch-long strips, and separately stitch together the 6, 26-inch-long strips. Set aside.

Lay down scrap newspaper to prevent the ink from bleeding through. On a scrap of blue fabric, make some practice stamps until you get the look you want, practicing with the amount of ink to use and how you want the pentacles to look. When you're happy with how they look, stamp the blue rectangle with pentacles. Remember to leave a little extra space around the edges for seams and hems. Set the ink with an iron if necessary according to the directions on the package.

Right sides together, stitch the completed blue field to the shorter stripe section to make a 26-inch-long rectangle. Right sides together, stitch the long section of stripes to this section, the stripe on the bottom of the flag being red. Hem the flag all the way around and trim any threads. If you wish to hang it on a rod, make a fabric tube or series of loops from leftover fabric.

PENNY RUG CANDLE MAT

Originally, "penny" rugs were made entirely from scrap fabric circles stitched together, but today's popular version places the "pennies" to the outer edges where they form an interesting border around a central design. In a Pagan spin on this old favorite, each of the 13 tabs bears a lovely full moon to represent the 13 moons of the year. The center is adorned with a simple pentacle, but this can be changed to any embroidered design you like, such as your coven's name, a triple moon, and nature motifs, and you can choose another color combination if you don't want to use green. Hand-dyed felts and threads add another dimension of texture, too.

YOU'LL NEED:

    ¼ yard of black wool felt
    Small piece of ivory wool felt
    6-inch-wide piece of medium green wool felt
    Scissors
    White sewing pencil

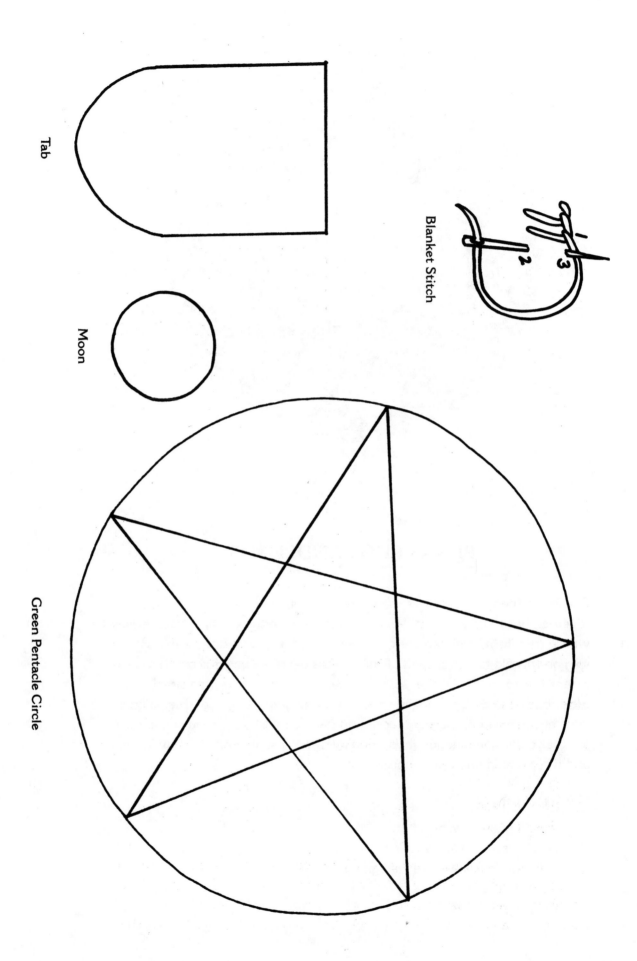

Tab

Blanket Stitch

Moon

Penny Rug Candlemat Patterns

Green Pentacle Circle

74

Embroidery floss or #5 perle cotton, 1 skein each
of tan and dark green
#5 embroidery needle
Black sewing thread or fabric adhesive

Cut 2, 9-inch circles and 13 tabs from the black felt. Cut 13, 1-inch circles from the ivory felt and the 6-inch pentacle from the green felt using the pattern provided. Trace the pentagram onto the green felt using the white sewing pencil.

Stitch all the ivory moons to the black tabs using blanket stitch and 3 strands of the tan floss, centering them in the curved end of the tab and leaving about $5/16$ inch all the way around each moon. Center the green circle on one of the 9-inch black circles and stitch the edges of the green circle down to the black circle using blanket stitch and 3 strands of the green floss.

Lay out the second black circle and arrange the tabs around the edges so that all 13 are evenly spaced with about $5/8$ inch of each tab inside the circle and the corners just touching. Baste in place with black thread or fabric adhesive.

Center the other black circle on top, sandwiching the ends of the tabs inside, and stitch the black circles together around the edge using blanket stitch and 6 strands of either floss color (your choice). Embroider the pentacle on the green circle using either split or chain stitch and 6 strands of the green floss, stitching through both layers of the black felt.

MYSTERY HOODS

These hoods that enable you to see out but don't allow others to see your face are extremely effective for a dramatic ritual presentation. Masks can be unnerving enough, but when presented with a being whose face appears to be gone completely, the effect for Samhain or Yule is chill-inducing.

YOU'LL NEED:

¼ yard sheer black fabric
½ yard medium-weight black knit fabric
¼ yard black heavy interfacing
Scissors
Sewing machine
Black thread

Cut out all pieces, making the face piece from the sheer panel so you can see through it. Cut one front edge from the interfacing.

Right sides together, stitch the two halves of the hood together, leaving the face area open. Hem the raw bottom edge. Wrong sides together,

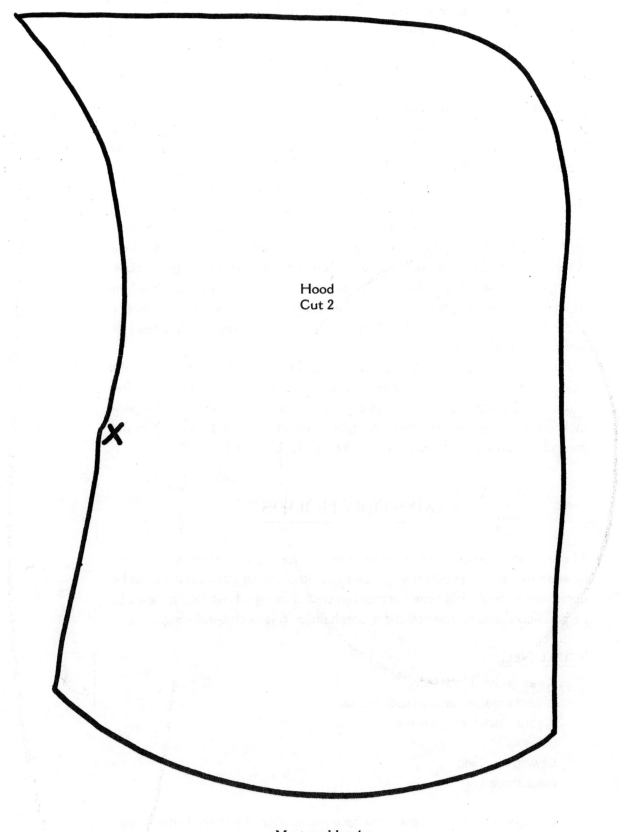

Hood
Cut 2

Mystery Hood

Mystery Hood

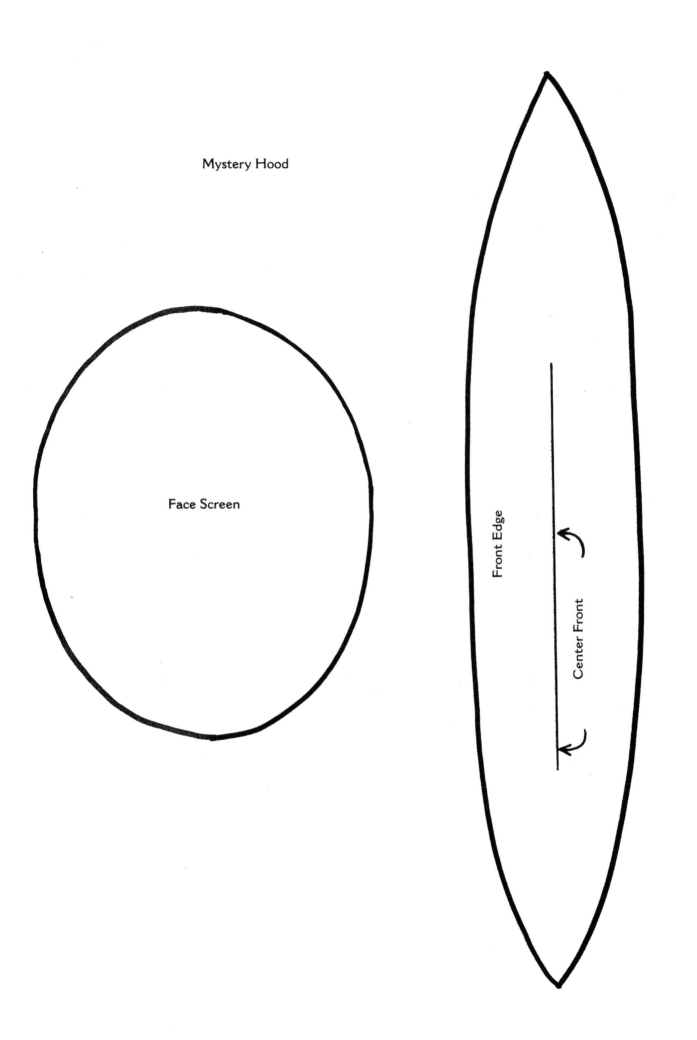

Face Screen

Front Edge

Center Front

match the interfacing with the front edge piece and fold in half lengthwise so the interfacing is inside. Right sides together, baste this to the face edge of the hood. Pin the sheer panel in place and stitch all layers together so that all seams are inside the completed hood. Gently press all seams away from the face following the fabric's recommended heat setting. Overcast stitch the inner seams if needed to keep them away from the wearer's face.

RESOURCES

e-Quilter.com
5455 Spine Road, Suite E
Boulder, CO 80301
(877) FABRIC-3 [323-7423]; www.equilter.com

An interesting variety of unusual quilting fabrics and especially novelty prints. Check out their wide selection of African, batik, and other import fabrics with motifs of interest to Pagans, such as cowrie shells.

Hancock's of Paducah
3841 Hinkleville Rd
Paducah, KY, 42001
(800) 845-8723; www.hancocks-paducah.com

A fantastic selection of quilting and home decorating fabrics, as well as sewing notions, patterns, and books. They offer some novelty fabrics I've never seen anywhere else, and their color catalogs are free.

Homespun Hearth
36 Apogee Circle
San Pedro, CA 90732
(866) 346-0414; www.homespunhearth.com

Great selection of real wool felt for making penny rugs and other crafts. Aside from plain colors, they also offer hand-dyed felt for a yummy designer look. Also carries other fabrics and supplies for "homespun" rustic crafts.

Tutu.com
P.O. Box 472287
Charlotte, NC 28247
(704) 542-2433; www.tutu.com/netnotions.html

Everything you need to make costume pieces and accessories, including specialty fabrics, glues, fasteners, hard-to-find notions, boning, and specialty items like feathers, flowers, and rhinestones.

5

Beads

I don't know what it is about beads, but the darn little things are just plain addictive. If you've done any beadwork, you probably know what I mean—once you get a few, you want to look at all the other colors. Your mind starts dreaming about what you could make with those . . . then you start looking at some different styles—that dichroic glass just begs to be used somewhere. Then there's some in the new arrivals you can't live without. Yes, my house is filled with beads, why do you ask?

I started out as a teenager learning seed bead techniques from the Miwok Indians in Yosemite, spending long hours after school making earrings and little beaded dolls. Later I picked up how to make earrings with headpins and eyepins, and in the past few years have been riding the stranded wire and crimp bead wave that's become such a big hit with jewelry makers. Along the way I've experimented with a lot of different beads.

It's astonishing to flip through a catalog and find literally thousands of different beads of every size, shape, and material imaginable. It's so hard to pick my favorite kind, and if you're a bead nut too you'll understand why! Glass is formed into tiny seed beads, fun pressed shapes, and miniature dichroic works of art. Gemstones are cut and polished into random chips or perfect spheres, or can be carved into animals, tubes, Celtic knots, or more. Shells are used in their natural form or shaped and carved, as are animal bones both small and large. Metal can be molded into anything imaginable, from simple balls to elaborate dangling charms, and can consist of inexpensive pewter or pure, precious gold. Wood, ceramics, polymer clay, coconut shells, betel nuts . . . anything durable enough to keep its shape when a hole is put through it can and probably has been made into a lovely bead. The original "rosary" necklace was created with beads made from boiled and pressed rose petals, for example. The possibilities are endless!

The techniques used to string this amazing array of beads is almost as diverse. For the purpose of this chapter, however, I've kept to some basic techniques. Nevertheless some have a bit of a tricky twist to them later in the chapter where you will find the more difficult projects. We start out with some very simple stringing on wire to make Wine Glass Charms and Crochet Stitch Markers, then move on to seed beads and other miniatures such as tiny button pearls for some stringing and stitching techniques. For the grand finale a guest artist has graciously allowed me to present her Beaded Goddess Doll project that uses both seed and pressed glass beads as well as wirework using sterling silver jeweler's wire and charms.

Luckily, beads are usually rather small and don't take up much storage space. Only one or two small storage cabinets are required for all your wire, tools, and beads. Oh, but I forgot about the large tackle box under my desk for the seed bead supplies. And there are a few things in my general craft storage bins, too . . . and there's a container of shells in the bedroom . . . and that little bag of quartz crystals I found next to the veggie seeds inside the buffet . . . uh oh. Well . . . it'll be at least 25 years until you get to that point. Perhaps.

WINE GLASS CHARMS

If your group uses individual glasses for your events or rituals, these colorful beaded accents make it easy to tell who belongs to which glass. Using deity or symbolic charms make them even more meaningful in a spiritual gathering of friends.

The Crafty Witch

> 4-mm split rings
> Brass or silver charms
> 1¼-inch memory wire hoops
> Assorted glass beads

Attach the split rings to the brass charms, then set aside. Choose a different color scheme for each charm, and set aside various beads in color groups—you can use either completely random beads or symmetrical beads like the ones in my examples. Make sure to use smaller beads next to the charm so that it's not obscured. Thread on 3 or 4 beads (depending on size), then add the charm, then 3 or 4 beads. That's all there is to it, simply place the finished hoops on each wine glass.

CROCHET STITCH MARKERS

Pretty glass novelty beads help you find your place as you crochet, especially important if you're doing spiral crochet in the round. Just slip a looped marker through your last stitch and the beads will keep it from coming back out. You can use any beads you like, just be sure they're drilled from top to bottom so that they hang properly when in use. Make lightweight ones for fine work and heavier markers for sport weight, worsted, or bulky.

YOU'LL NEED:

> 2-inch headpins (not the soft gold kind)
> Several top-drilled goddess or other beads
> Several lotus-shaped pressed glass beads
>   (often called "tulips," optional)
> Assorted 4-mm to 8-mm glass beads
> Round-nose pliers

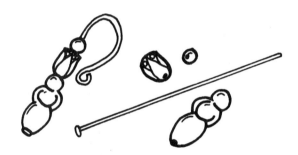

Crochet Stitch
Markers

Slide your beads onto the headpin, first placing the goddess bead, then the lotus bead on her "head," then 1 or 2 small glass beads. The beads should total about 1 inch in length, leaving about 1 inch of headpin empty. Use more beads for heavyweight yarns, and fewer or lighter beads for fine crochet thread.

Make a tight loop at the end of the headpin, enclosing it completely. Bend the top of the headpin over into a gentle U-shape as shown in the illustration.

FOUR ELEMENTS BADGE LANYARD

Office buildings, trade shows, conventions . . . they all use name or security badges, and getting stuck with a cheapo ugly lanyard is a drag. This sparkly confection, dripping with interesting beads (and magic), isn't very hard to make, especially if you've worked with wire and crimp beads before. Where's the magic come in? The lanyard is divided up into four quarters, each one representing a different element, and is arranged according to ceremonial magic (Air, Earth, Fire, Water). Charge it, wear it so that Air is on your right shoulder, and your lanyard doubles as a powerful protective spell.

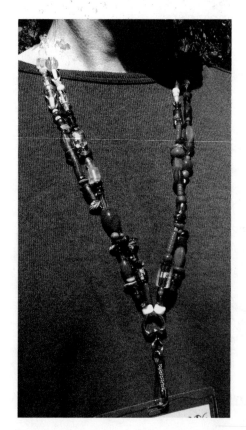

YOU'LL NEED:

7 × 7 strand coated .024 beading wire

Wire cutters

Crimp beads

Needle nose pliers

Lanyard hardware

Bead board (optional)

Assorted 3-mm to 15-mm beads in yellow, white, brown, green, red, and blue (you can also add a few orange and a few aqua if you like)

2 white or black glass crow beads

2, 9-mm (or 1, 18-mm) yellow dichroic glass beads

1, 20-mm brown and green agate bead

1, 18-mm orange dichroic glass spiral bead

1, 19-mm blue lampwork glass fish bead

The basic form of this necklace is 2 strands joined in 4 places by larger beads and terminating at the top of the lanyard hardware. The beads that are next to the 4 large "join" beads must be smaller in diameter (about 3 or 4 mm) so that the strands will lay next to each other nicely—"E" beads or similar are good here. Also use smaller beads of this size at the back center so it doesn't feel lumpy on your neck and your fancier beads are more easily seen in the front.

The 4 sections are divided up by color and bead materials. Air is yellow, white, and clear with some star-shape beads. Earth is green and brown with some stone, nut, and wooden beads. Fire is red (and orange if you add it) and primarily glass with some dyed bone. Water is blue and white (and aqua if you add it) and contains some shell beads—the holes were too small in the freshwater pearls I had, but if you can find some with larger holes to admit the wire they would be lovely in that section.

Cross Stitch "Witch's Brew" Mug

Needlepoint Sacred Lotus (pink)

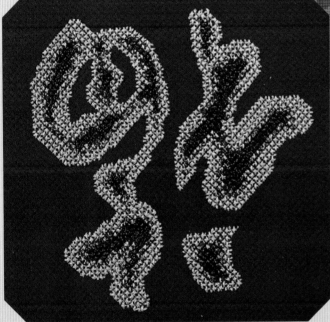

Cross Stitch Chinese Good Luck Hanger

"Magic in Progress" Door Hanger

Assisi Candle Hugger

Shisa Mirror
Altar Cloth

Pomegranate
and Pentacle
Blackwork
Border

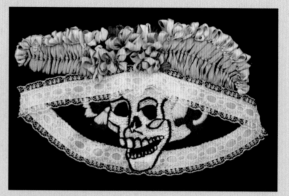

Ribbon Embroidery Catrina

Or Nue Hathor Panel

Stumpwork Lord
of the Woods

Crewel Herb Neckline

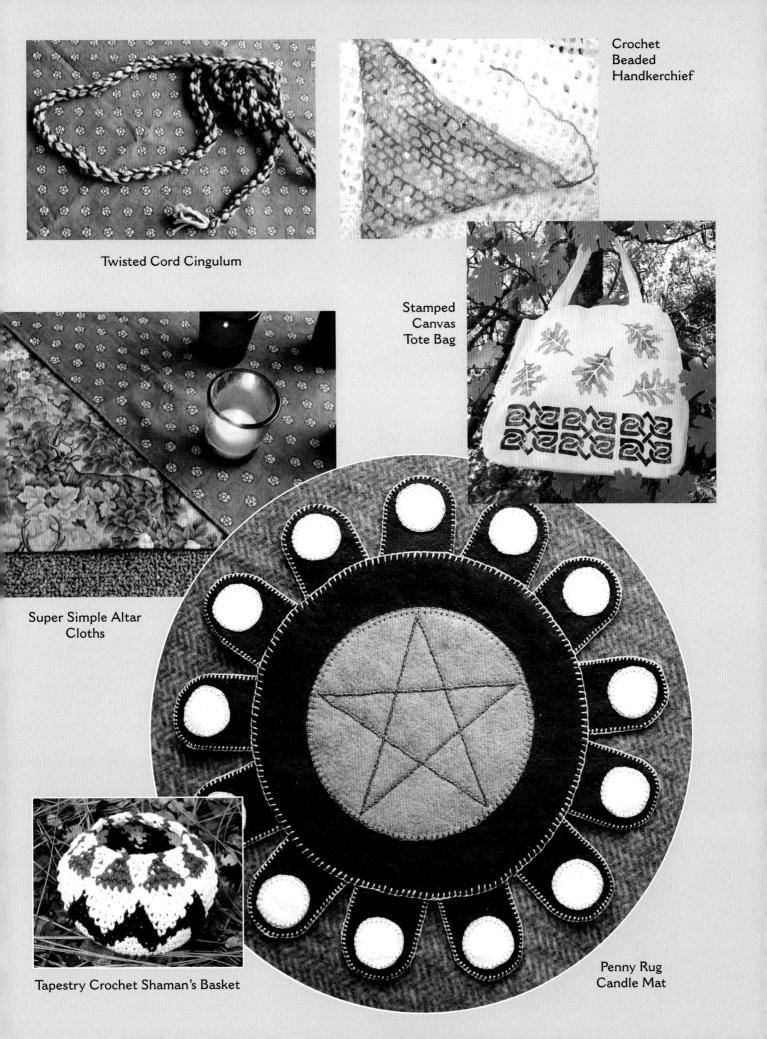

Twisted Cord Cingulum

Crochet Beaded Handkerchief

Stamped Canvas Tote Bag

Super Simple Altar Cloths

Tapestry Crochet Shaman's Basket

Penny Rug Candle Mat

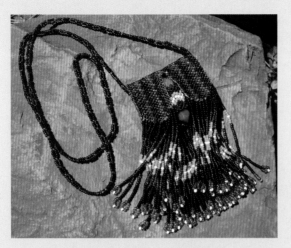

Peyote Stitch Crystal Pouch

Seed Bead Edgings

Wine Glass Charms

Bead
Goddess

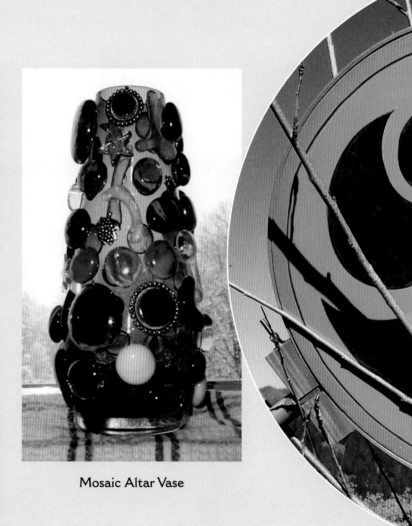

Mosaic Altar Vase

Nice Fat
Charm Bracelet

Quilt Hoop
Frame Drum

Embossed Copper Foil Pentacle

Wire Labyrinth Path Pendant

Crocheted Wire
Faerie Circlet

Embellished Devotional Shelf (bottom)

Embellished Devotional Shelf (top)

Victorian Recycled
Card Ornaments
(finished)

Victorian Recycled Card Ornaments (prep)

Sunny May Day Gift Bag

Golden Paperclay Staff Head

3-D Tole Pictures

Potato Stamped
Garden Stakes

Gourd
Devotion
Bowl

Wheel of the Year
Wreath

Herbal Cold-Process Soaps

Beeswax
Ointments

Decorated Leather
Pet Collar

Rattlesnake
Rattle

Tooled Leather Athenian Coin Paperback Cover

Porcupine Quill Oak Leaf Design

Cut 2 pieces of wire at least 30 inches long. Attach both strands to the top of the lanyard hardware (split ring, swivel clip, etc.), securing them each with 2 crimp beads to ensure that the wire doesn't slip and the lanyard is extremely durable (a cascade of beads onto the floor is a bad thing). Slip one of the crow beads over both of these joins so both wires are going through this bead.

Begin randomly threading the brown and green Earth beads on ONE of the strands. Finish at 2½ inches with one or two small beads, then add the large agate joiner bead. Continue with a couple of smaller beads and keep threading on brown and green Earth beads to 7 inches.

Switch to the yellow and white Air beads, threading them onto the wire in a random fashion until you reach 10 inches. Remember to make the last couple of beads about 3 or 4 mm in diameter. Add the yellow dichroic joiner bead(s) and continue with the Air beads to about 13½ inches. Add about ¾ of an inch of small beads, switch to the small blue and white Water beads for another ¾ of an inch, and move to the larger random Water beads. At 17½ inches thread on the blue fish joiner bead, head first so it looks up when worn, then continue with Water beads to the 21½-inch mark.

Switch to the red Fire beads and add them randomly to the 25-inch mark. Add the orange dichroic swirl bead, then continue adding Fire beads until you reach 28 inches. Check to be sure the large joiner beads will approximately line up when the lanyard/necklace is worn. If they're way off, you may need to restring part of this strand. When it's right, add the matching crow bead and crimp the wire onto the lanyard hardware with a small amount of extra slack in the wire.

Now begin stringing the other strand in the same manner, using smaller beads when next to the larger joiner bead in each section so that the two strands lay the same when worn. When you reach this larger bead, simply run the wire through it and continue on the other side as a separate strand again. You will end up with this pattern: crow bead, 2 strands; Earth bead, 2 strands; Air bead, 2 strands around the back; Water bead, 2 strands; Fire bead, 2 strands; crow bead.

Adjust the second strand so that the slack in the first strand is taken up and both strands lay evenly and flat for a uniform look. Attach the second wire to the lanyard hardware as before and crimp off, threading any wire tails up through the beads to conceal them and protect the wearer.

NICE FAT CHARM BRACELET

These fun bracelets are popular and are a delight to shake and play with. Yours has special meaning, too; when mixed with colorful mundane beads, the sacred charms can hide in plain sight if you don't want to be too obvious about your path in public. Create yours in a particular color scheme, go wild and use whatever mix you like, or even close your eyes and let Spirit choose the next bead. A perfect project for your group, especially if you all bring beads and pour them in the same bowl. I found some really great charms at the craft store—the chalice was in a pack of "wine glass charms" and the flat celestial ones were in the "do it yourself greeting card" section.

YOU'LL NEED:

Large charm bracelet with open links (use one size larger than what you usually wear)
2-inch headpins and eyepins colored to match the base chain (gold or silver)
Assorted symbolic charms such as a chalice, star, pentacle, ankh, etc.
Assorted beads, between about 3 mm and 15 mm
Small round needle-nose pliers

Leave 2 empty links at both ends of the bracelet so the clasp fastens properly and is easier to close. Each link will get 4 headpins attached to it, 2 on the top of the link and 2 on the bottom—this is for even distribution of the beaded pins. Look at the loop as if it were a sideways "O," then notice the links connecting at each side. Your headpins will go in pairs on the top and bottom of the "O."

Open the bracelet and lay it out flat. Using a headpin, pick up an assortment of beads—smaller ones at the top, larger ones at the bottom. If the large bead has a hole so big that the head slips through it, you'll need to place a small bead at the bottom and then add the larger bead on top of it. Put on 5 or 6 beads, then cut off any excess pin, leaving about ⅜-inch of empty pin. With your round pliers, bend the pin just above the last bead at about a 45-degree angle, then make an open loop by curling the rest of the pin around the round pliers so that it fits over the bracelet link. Slip the loop onto the bracelet link and close the loop. The headpin loop should be large enough that the pin dangles freely.

Make a few eyepins in advance by opening up the pre-formed loop at the end of the pin and adding a charm, then closing the loop. As you did with the headpins, add beads, cut off any excess pin, and make a loop to attach the eyepin to the bracelet. Intersperse these charm eyepins with the headpins randomly throughout the bracelet.

Continue working along the bracelet, adding beaded headpins and eye-pins, 2 on each side of every link for a total of 4 pins per link. Have fun mixing up the colors and adding beads randomly for a wild and whimsical look. Remember to leave the last couple of links empty for fastening the clasp.

SEED BEAD EDGINGS

Add some shimmer and elegance to your ritual robes, altar cloth, pouches, prayer shawl, or other fabric items with these simple edgings. Feel free to play with the colors, change the beads at the end of the fringe, and otherwise make these a reflection of your personality.

YOU'LL NEED:

- Assorted #11 seed beads (I used silver-lined red, dark metallic copper, and metallic grey)
- 6-mm hematite puffy star beads (or your choice of bead, for fringe edging only)
- #12 beading needle (or your favorite size)
- Needle threader (optional)
- Sewing thread
- Scissors
- Small piece of beeswax

Cut an 18-inch length of sewing thread and run it through the beeswax several times. This will help prevent fraying and tangling. Thread the needle and tie a knot in the end of the thread unless you are working on the selvage (woven) edge of your fabric, in which case you will need to take a couple of tiny stitches next to where you're starting and then conceal the thread "tail" inside your stitching as you work.

For the fringe edging: Plunge the needle downward through the fabric where you want the fringe to start or, if you're working on the selvage, stitch very close to the edge of the fabric. Thread the desired beads on the needle, then thread several more (an odd number) if you want a loop at the

end of your fringe, or thread on your large bead. Go back up through the initial beads only, not the odd number at the end, and draw up the loop. If thread is showing, catch the bead at the center of the loop and gently tug on the thread to "snug up" the strand. Don't make it too tight, however, or your fringe will be stiff and not hang nicely. Move over about 3 millimeters and work another strand of fringe in the same way.

For the netted edging: Plunge the needle downward through the fabric as described above. String about 25 seed beads (it must be an odd number) and go back up through the fabric, making a graceful, half-circle loop. To make it easier to find the center of the loop on the return trip, the middle bead should be a different color. Repeat until the end of the fabric is reached. Go back through the last loop to the center bead, then exit the loop. String another 25 or 30 beads, then go through the center bead of the next loop. Repeat, making this netted pattern, until the end of the row is reached. Go back through half of the last loop as you did at the beginning of this row and tie off the thread.

LOOM-WOVEN HATBAND

Bay laurel leaves, the traditional symbol of wisdom and knowledge, form a magic charm that's hidden in plain sight. The black beads forming the background have a matte finish that adds an extra dimension of texture when contrasted with the glossy green of the leaves. It looks best on a dark-color hat—try playing with the background color so that it looks best on your favorite chapeau.

YOU'LL NEED:

Flexible measuring tape
Sewing thread
Scissors
Small beading loom
1 hank each #11/0 seed beads:
    light green
    medium green
    dark green
    matte black
Small piece of beeswax
#12 beading needles
Needle threader
Scrap of thin suede leather
Pen or pencil
Craft glue

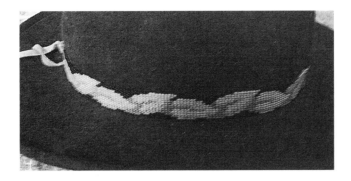

Measure the diameter of your hat where the hatband will lay, and subtract about 2 inches. This is the approximate measurement of the finished beaded part of the hatband. Add 8 inches to this measurement and cut 13 lengths of thread to this length. Tie all the strands together with an overhand knot at one end and lay it over the thread-holder screw on your beading loom's spool. Distribute half the threads on each side of the screw and pull the bundle up in your hands so they're all even. Tie another knot in the other end of the thread bundle and place this over the other end of your loom. Wind up one end of the loom so that you are starting near one of the knots and the other end of the thread bundle is wrapped around the spool. Use your fingernail, a stiletto, a toothpick, or other tool to lay the threads evenly in the loom's slots.

Cut an 18-inch length of thread and run it through the beeswax a few times to help it resist tangling. Thread it through the needle and then tie the end to the leftmost thread on your loom (rightmost, if you're left-handed). Remember, the wrapped up end of the loom is farthest away from you. Pick up the beads on your needle according to the chart, left to right (if right-handed). Slide them to the end of the thread, then push them up between the threads on the loom with your finger. Stitch back through this row of beads *on top* of the loom threads to lock the beads in place. Run the thread back under the loom threads and pick up the next row of beads.

Repeat this process until the beadwork is very close to the end of your original hat measurement minus 2 inches. Finish at the end of a leaf, stitching extra black background as needed to make the leaf stand alone at the end of the work. Make sure your beadwork does not exceed your measurement! Tie off the end of the thread as you tied on at the beginning. Carefully remove your beadwork from the loom by slipping the knots off the loom screws and set aside.

Measure the finished width of your beadwork and add about ⅛ inch. Cut 2 circles this diameter from the thin leather, then cut 2 tie strips ⅜-inch wide by 6 inches long. Fold the leather circles in half, right sides in (if there is a front and back to your leather) and mark this line.

Clip the knots off the ends of the beadwork and find the center thread. Stitch this thread through the center of the leather on the marked line,

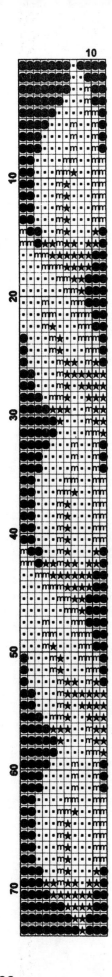

Fabric: Loom 14–9, White
                12w × 74h Stitches
Size: 14 Count, 0-³/₄w × 8-¹/₈h in

Floss Used for Full Stitches:

Symbol	Strands	Type	Number	Color
·	2	Cust Bead	11SB182	Light Green
m	2	Cust Bead	11SB183	Medium Green
★	2	Cust Bead	11SB186	Dark Green
●	2	Cust Bead	11SB109M	Matte Black

The Crafty Witch

making sure that it's on the opposite side of the leather from the beadwork. Continue stitching the loom threads through the leather on the line, including the thread knotted onto the loom thread that runs through the beads. Draw up all these threads evenly and tie another overhand knot within the diameter of the leather circle (fold it in half to check). Repeat for the other end of the beadwork.

Spread a small amount of glue on the inside of the leather circle and lay one end of the leather tie inside this circle as well. Clip off any excess thread and press the halves of the leather circle together tightly until they bond securely. Repeat for the other end to complete the hatband. Allow to dry completely before using the leather ties to fit the hatband to your hat. If it tends to slide off your hat or otherwise shift around in an undesirable manner, you can tack it down directly to your hat at several points with matching thread.

FLAT PEYOTE STITCH ISIS BANNER OR PENDANT

You can actually make this design in four different sizes, depending on what beads you use! If you use 11/0 seed beads, you'll get a necklace; pony or E beads and you'll have a small design to hang over your altar; crow beads will give you a door hanger; larger wooden beads will create a big wall banner. The hieroglyphs read "Praise Aset (Isis)" and depict the goddess in a white linen dress with wings that fan ankhs, the symbol of life.

You'll Need:

Beads in the following colors, your choice of size:
  1000 natural/light tan
  170 white
  170 tan
  80 brown
  65 metallic gold
  40 red or scarlet
  35 turquoise or aqua
  35 royal blue
  30 black
Sewing thread, #10 crochet thread, or string
Needle the appropriate size for your beads and thread
Scissors
Wooden dowel and string or ribbon (if making one of the
  larger designs)

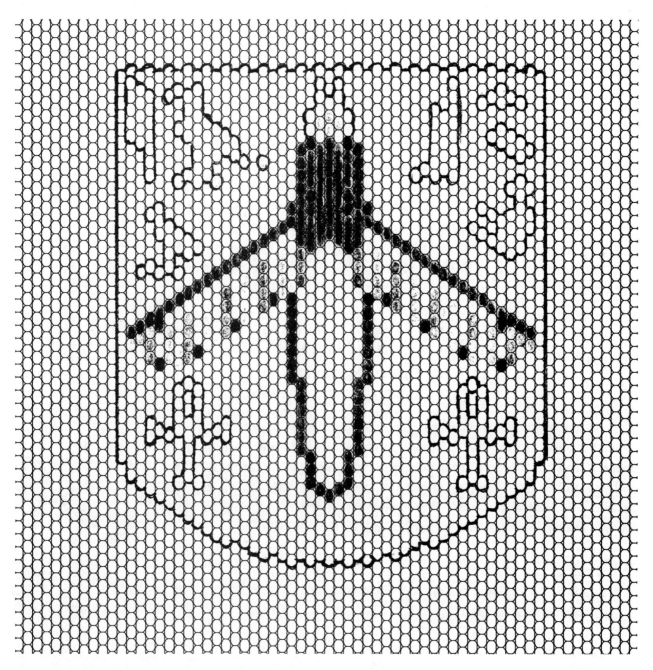

Peyote Isis Beadwork

Starting at the top, pick up 46 natural/light tan beads. Go back through bead #43 and pull the thread up tight so that the last bead (#46) sits on top of bead #44 and bead #45 is on the end. Weave back through the previous row, picking up tan beads as needed to complete the row (you will need to use 2 gold beads near the center of the design for the tips of her headdress). You will now have an alternating pattern of 1-2-1-2 beads all along this row.

The Crafty Witch

Continue weaving back and forth in this brickwork pattern, weaving the thread in and out of the beads as necessary at the end of each row so that you are able to add the first bead of the next row properly. Follow the chart to add the various colors required to make the pattern.

When you approach the bottom of the banner, weave the threads into the ends as necessary to reduce the ends and form the curve. If making the necklace, see the instructions in the Crystal Pouch project for beading a strap so that you can wear it. Any larger design can be hung by whip stitching the top edge to a dowel and attaching string or ribbon to the ends of the dowel.

PEYOTE STITCH CRYSTAL POUCH

This interesting amulet pouch incorporates a gemstone crystal by covering it with beads and stitching it right into the front of the pouch. The zigzag pattern represents energy movement, and the unusual split front to the pouch shows off the crystal beautifully. If you've never done peyote stitch before, you might want to try this project after you've had a bit of experience.

YOU'LL NEED:

Thin gemstone crystal (I used an aventurine necklace and removed the silver finding)
Nail polish remover (optional)
1 hank each 10/0 or 11/0 seed beads:
    black
    iridescent red
    iridescent blue
Small amount of 10/0 or 11/0 seed beads of your choice (I used medium green and pearl ivory)
Beeswax
Sewing thread
Scissors
Needle threader
Beading needle

If you're using a faceted necklace crystal like I did, you'll need to remove the silver bail finding that holds the crystal so it can be worn as a necklace. Most likely the adhesive is an acetone-based epoxy, so simply dip the bail in some nail polish remover until it can be removed from the gemstone crystal. If it still won't come off, try various solvents until you find one that works, or buy a crystal without a bail (which can be harder to find).

Once the crystal is free and has been washed to remove the solvent and any traces of glue, begin beading around it. Begin by cutting a 24-inch length of sewing thread (approximate length), then run it through the beeswax until it's lightly and evenly coated. The wax helps to prevent the thread from tangling and makes it "grab" a little so your finished work is tighter.

Thread the beading needle and pick up one bead from the center color of the band that will go around the crystal (in my example it's pearl ivory). Tie this bead on to the end of the thread leaving a tail about 2 inches long. Pick up enough beads to go around the crystal—it must be an odd number, and a little bit of slack in the circle of beads is better than an exact fit or a tight fit. Run the needle through the bead tied to the end of the thread. This is the beginning center row of the crystal band.

Pick up 1 green bead (or your choice of color). Begin the round peyote stitch by skipping the next ivory bead and going through the next bead with the needle. Continue stitching beads in the colors and pattern that you like, to a total of about 4 rows. Weave the thread back through to the tied-on bead, and work in the same way out from the center again another 4 or so rows. Weave the thread back to the beginning, and tie it off using the starting tail. Clip the thread. If the crystal is loose and wants to slip out of the beadwork, use a bit of glue in the back (where the thread tail is) to secure it.

When you come to the end of your thread, you have a couple of choices regarding how to add a new thread. One way is to weave the end back through your work and either leave it or knot it to the edge of your work, then weave in or knot the new thread at the edge and work your way back over to where you can pick up your stitching. Another way is to very securely square knot the new thread to the end of the old thread. This can slip out or make a thicker area inside the beads you're trying to sew through, but it's a more invisible join.

Re-thread the needle with another length of waxed thread. Pick up 79 beads and tie the first one on, leaving a tail about 2 inches long. Assuming you are working the same pattern as my pouch, it will be 2 black, 2 blue, 2 red, repeat until bead number 79, which is black. Go through the tied black bead, pick up blue, skip the next bead, and go through the first blue bead to begin the zigzag pattern. The center back row will be 1 bead thicker than the other zigzags—simply add an extra black bead as needed to continue the pattern. Continue in this pattern for ½ inch.

Gently fold the beaded loop so that the thread tail is in the center back. Note where the center front will fall, and continue beading around to this point. Now as you work, incorporate the beaded crystal, meshing the last row of the crystal's beadwork with the last row of the pouch. Thread the needle through the stitches on the crystal, then continue with the pouch beadwork out the other side to unite them.

As you work, be careful to align the beads to continue the pouch pattern—try to avoid puckering and skipped stitches. In the last couple of rows that incorporate the crystal, you may find that there's been some unintentional distortion. You can realign the zigzag pattern as needed in the couple of rows that are hidden behind the crystal if necessary. Continue the zigzag pattern up until the crystal is centered on the body of the pouch.

Lay the pouch down, gently folding it so that it forms a flat packet with the crystal centered on the front. You are now starting the flap of the pouch which is a continuation of the back. The flap consists of the 33 beads in the back, with the wider black zigzag forming the center of this back piece. If it's not in the exact center, that's fine—you'll be forming the split on the black zigzag, so you have a few rows to fudge the positioning of the split.

Following the drawing, when you reach the edge of the flap, reverse your stitching direction and continue the peyote stitch pattern back the other direction. Up to this point you've been working in a spiral—now you'll be stitching back and forth in rows. Again, following the drawing, when you reach the edge of the flap, reverse and go back the other way, continuing the pattern for ½ inch.

When you reach the center of the flap, reverse your stitching direction as before to begin forming one half of the split in the flap (16 beads wide each). Continue for 1 inch, then skip the first and last beads on each row as you work to form a V at the end of the flap. Return to the center and repeat for the other half of the flap, making sure the flap ends are the same length.

If you find that you've accidentally made the flap 1 bead short or wide, don't rip the whole thing out! When you come to the edge that's not working out quite right, all you need to do is add the bead that sits on top of the previous row (the first bead of the new row). Stitch through the previous edge bead, then weave the thread in the next couple of beads so that you come out through the same previous edge bead. Now stitch into the end bead sitting on top and you're ready to work the next row. Repeat at the other end of the row if necessary. That's one nice thing about peyote stitch, it's very forgiving since you can weave your thread around through the rows until it comes out where you need it to.

Now work the fringe on the flap, which on my example consists of 9 black, 9 blue, 3 green, 1 ivory pearl, 3 green, 9 blue, nine black, then the loop at the end is 4 red, 1 ivory pearl, 4 red. If you want a more exaggerated V-shape design, make the previous pattern the center fringe strand, and as you work toward the edges remove one black bead from the top of each strand.

Stitch the bottom of the pouch closed by going through the bottom edge beads and working the fringe at the same time. Use the same fringe pattern as given above along the bottom of the pouch (or do a different pattern if you prefer). As each strand of fringe is done, stitch through the bottom beads of the pouch to close it up.

For the beaded strap, use 2 colors of your choice from the palette already used, such as blue and black, red and ivory, etc., or use the pattern pictured which is 4 blue, 1 red, 4 black, 1 red, 4 blue, and so on. Securely attach your waxed thread to one top edge of the pouch, then pick up 3 of your main color, 1 of the accent color, 3 of the main color, etc. until the strand is about an inch longer than the desired finished length (I made mine 30 inches long). Securely stitch the other end to the opposite edge of the pouch leaving a little slack in the line of beads—do not make the strand tight! Now pick up your main color and stitch through the accent color bead, repeating this pattern the length of the strand. This creates a "4-drop" peyote stitch strand. Tie off securely and clip thread. If the regular waxed sewing thread doesn't prove to be strong enough (durability depends on thread brand, possible thread batch flaws, and amount of pouch use), try using doubled strands, nylon beading thread, or very thinly split artificial sinew.

BEADED GODDESS DOLLS

This project appears courtesy of the Arizona artisan Ronda Kivett, who says: "I have been intrigued by the many bead embroidery goddess dolls that have been springing up, and wanted to design something around that theme that had a contemporary twist. Working with wire has really opened my mind to a whole new creative design process. Wire is very versatile and can be shaped into many different forms. Adding beads can bring the form to life by creating depth and texture. Once finished, she can be admired from both sides if you choose to hang her in a sunny window to reflect light." You can see more of Ronda's beautiful designs by visiting www.kivett-studio.com.

YOU'LL NEED:

- 18-gauge craft or silver wire
- 24-gauge craft or silver wire
- Diagonal wire cutters
- Needle-nose pliers
- Assorted glass beads, 4 mm to 10 mm in size
- Assorted 11/0 seed beads
- 2 hand-shape charms
- 1 face bead (purchased or handmade)
- 4 leaf-shape pressed glass beads

If you are not an experienced wire worker, it's economical to experiment with craft wire before moving on to the more expensive sterling silver

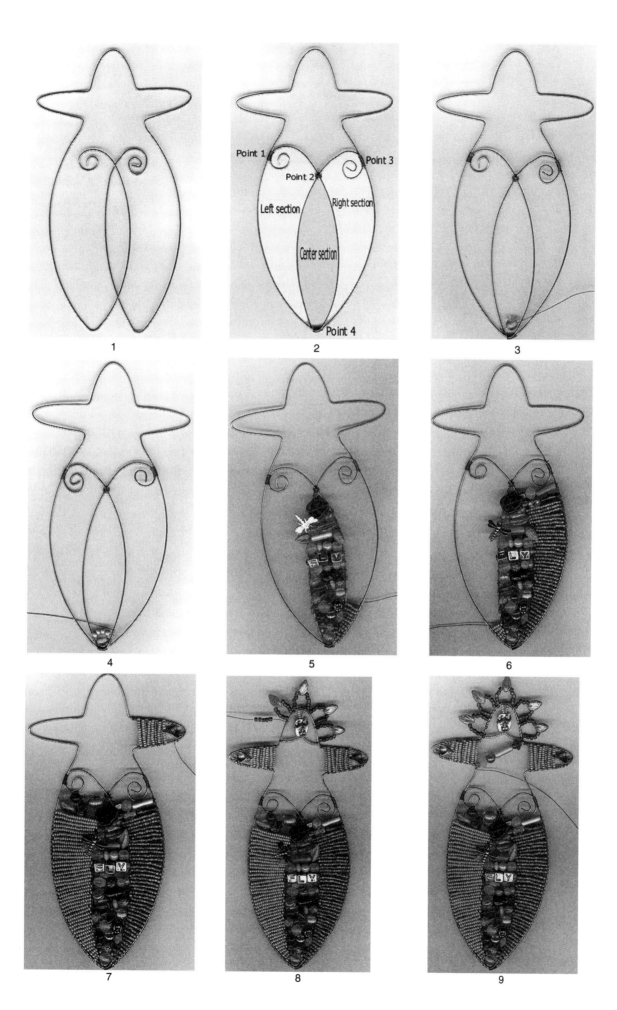

1

2

Point 1
Point 2
Point 3
Left section
Right section
Center section
Point 4

3

4

5

6

7

8

9

95

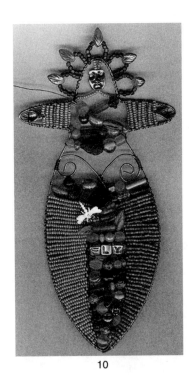

10

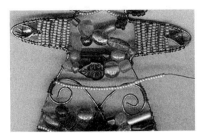

11

12

wire when you become more adept. When beading, work with a length of wire that you are comfortable with. If 36 inches is too long, start with 24 to 28 inches until you become adept in manipulating the wire. Longer lengths can easily become twisted or tangled, but you can avoid these problems with practice.

To create a 7-inch-tall goddess form, cut a 34-inch length of 18-gauge wire. Using the template in photo 1 as a guide, bend the wire to form the goddess frame, working symmetrically down the body. Photo 2 can also be used as a template to create a smaller 5½-inch goddess form if you choose not to make a 7-inch size, just trim away excess wire after shaping or begin with a shorter length of wire. Approximately 30 inches will make a 5½-inch form. Cut 4, 4-inch lengths of 24-gauge wire. Wrap the key points of the frame specified in photo 2 with the pieces of 24-gauge wire for strength.

Begin the wire wrapping on the center section by cutting a 36-inch length of 24-gauge wire. Wrap five times to secure in place at the lower left side of the center section. Thread a medium-size bead (4 mm–6 mm), then wrap the wire two times to secure to the left side of the center section (see photo 3). You will need to add more wire as you go while wrapping since it's difficult to work with a length longer than 36 inches due to tangling. To add wire, cut a length that you are comfortable with and wrap the end three or four times in the spot where you ran out of wire, then push the 2 separate wire coils together with the needle-nose pliers to compact them so there are no gaps between wraps. Begin stringing beads just as you had left off.

Thread on another medium-size bead, then wrap the wire securing to the right side to the center section. Repeat the process wrapping from one side of the center section to the other, wrapping to secure between adding various sized beads (see photo 4). If desired, several alphabet beads or charms can be inserted in this section to add a unique touch to your goddess. When the top of the center section is reached, wrap four times to secure, then cut away any excess 24-gauge wire.

Both the left and right side sections of the goddess frame can be filled in the same manner as the center section using #11/0 seed beads. Cut a 36-inch length of 24-gauge wire. Secure at the lower right outside section. Thread enough 11/0 seed beads to fill the space and wrap the wire to the frame of the center section by weaving the wire between the larger beads already in place. Thread more seed beads and wrap the wire one time around the outside of the section of the frame. Repeat this process wrapping from side to side and adding as many seed beads as needed to fill the space (see photo 5). Seed beads can be used to fill the entire section, or approximately 1 inch from the top of the section you can switch to larger beads (4 mm–10 mm in size) as shown in photo 6. When the top of the section is reached, wrap five times securely around the frame and trim the excess 24-gauge wire. Repeat this step to fill in the left outside section of the goddess frame with seed beads.

To complete the arm sections, cut 1, 18-inch length of 24-gauge wire. Secure the wire to the area between the neck and upper arm of the frame. Using 11/0 seed beads, thread on enough seed beads to fill the width of the arm section. Wrap the wire one time to the lower arm frame. Repeat the wrapping and threading process working toward the end of the arm. When the wrist area is reached, thread 3 seed beads, a hand charm, then 3 seed beads, and wrap along the hand area of the frame to secure. Lay the wire over the hand charm and secure by wrapping to the frame again (see photo 7). Repeat this step to complete the other arm.

To attach the face bead, cut a 24-inch length of 24-gauge wire and secure it to the left side neck curve of the frame. Thread 10 seed beads, the face bead, and 4 seed beads. Wrap the wire six times at the center top of the head of the frame. Thread 4 seed beads, go back through the face bead, thread 10 seed beads, and wrap the wire three times to the right side neck curve of the frame. Do not trim the excess wire.

Begin attaching the hair—thread 5 to 7 seed beads, 1 leaf bead, and 5 to 7 seed beads. Wrap the wire to the frame three times to create the hair loop. Repeat this step four more times to fill the head with hair loops as shown in photo 8.

To fill in the chest area, cut an 18-inch length of 24-gauge wire and secure to the right side between the neck and arm of the frame. Thread assorted-sized beads (4 mm to 10 mm in size) to fill the area diagonally and wrap the wire three times to the frame under the left arm above the waist area (see photo 9). Thread another length of assorted-size glass beads and secure the wire to the right side waist of the frame. Add 2 more lengths of beads at the waist, ending on the right side. Wrap three times to secure, then thread the wire with assorted-size glass beads and secure diagonally to the left side between the neck and arm (see photo 10). Trim excess wire.

To complete the goddess doll, cut a 10-inch length of 24-gauge wire and secure it to the left curl (shown as Point 1 in photo 2). Thread approximately 3 inches of size 11/0 seed beads (see photo 11), spiral the wire along the left curl of the frame working toward the right side curl (shown as Point 3 in photo 2) then wrap the wire five times to secure. Trim excess wire.

RESOURCES

Beaded Impressions
1750 30th Street, #167
Boulder, CO 80301
(303) 442-3473; www.abeadstore.com

Not the biggest selection, but they have some unusual colors and items that are difficult or impossible to find elsewhere, such as mini button pearls.

Fire Mountain Gems
One Fire Mountain Way
Grants Pass, OR 97526
(800) 355-2137; www.firemountaingems.com

For semiprecious gemstone beads, cabochons, or necklace sets, this is the first place to look. Fire Mountain specializes in gem beads, and has a complete selection of beads and findings as well in a huge, full-color catalog.

General Bead
637 Minna Street
San Francisco, CA 94103
(415) ALL-BEAD [255-2323]; www.genbead.com

This California-based bead shop carries unusual beads and metal charms that I've never seen anywhere else, at great prices. Well worth a look, especially if you need inexpensive stamped charms. I've bought from them for many years.

Rings & Things

P.O. Box 450

Spokane, WA 99210

(800) 366-2156; www.rings-things.com

I think the best feature of this company is the number of hard-to-find clasps, clips, and other items that no one else seems to have. This company also has interesting and unusual figural and handmade beads from all over the planet.

Shipwreck Beads

8560 Commerce Place Drive NE

Lacey, WA 98516

(800) 950-4232; www.shipwreck.com

My favorite online bead store, they always have an interesting and amazing selection of beads from around the world. Fast, friendly service and a full-color catalog the size of a small phone book are two more good reasons to check out these guys.

6

Glass

There seems to be something magical about glass! How amazing that a liquid can be cut and formed into various shapes and waterproof containers, and that a shard of it can be so dangerously sharp! Glass is actually a liquid, believe it or not, and it flows very, very slowly over hundreds of years. The stained glass windows in the great cathedrals of Europe are slowly becoming more fragile as their tops become thinner over time.

Another quality of this amazing material is seen, once again, in the stained glass window. Looking through stained glass windows at night, or from the outside of a church during the day perhaps, they appear dull, dark, and nearly colorless. But when the sun's light blazes behind the colorful panes, they spring to vibrant life, almost seeming to move and breathe on their own as living beings. A well-designed window can inspire one to the point of a religious experience, whether the subject matter is religious or not. I gasp at the intense beauty of an authentic Tiffany window that depicts nature to such an elevated degree that it becomes hyperreality . . . the trees, water, and flowers becoming holy visions, especially when illuminated by the life-giving sun.

Although not made from glass, the first project in this chapter is designed to be placed on window glass so that the pieces can glow within their own sacred light. As well, the frosted and embellished containers can be placed on a sunny windowsill to catch the light, or they can be used on the altar to add color and magical sparkle.

Mosaics are often made with ceramic tiles, but can also be made with broken dishes, glass tiles, beads, and molded glass shapes as well as other durable objects like seashells and stones. In this chapter, I've combined glass shapes and objects with various other materials to create four elemental "miniliths" for your outdoor sacred space. "Monolith" means "a large single block of stone," and a "megalith" is an even larger version in an ancient structure, such as those seen at Stonehenge in England. I wanted to do something a little special for my outdoor circle, and I had a lot of fun making the Cernunnos mosaic in my previous book, so I thought it would be an easy and delightful project to make a set of four miniliths that incorporate various materials, especially glass.

The glass was important because I love how it both reflects and refracts the sunlight, especially when transparent or translucent. There's a certain quality to this material, refined from simple silica sand, that is ephemeral, somewhat transitory in its fragility and liquidity, and almost something like a window to another world when used as a raw art material by an artisan. Imagine . . . simple silica sand transformed by fire into the amazing and versatile medium we know as glass. Just creating it is something like a small act of magic . . . working with it as an artist adds our own power and beauty as well.

EGYPTIAN WINDOW CLINGS

Not made of glass, but for your window glass! These reusable clings work on any flat glass surface, including in your home, car, or office. Their stained glass–like effect celebrates the beauty of these two solar Egyptian deities.

YOU'LL NEED:

DecoArt Liquid Rainbow colors:
    black or gold leading (your choice)
    primary yellow
    orange lollipop
    burgundy blast
Sheet of clear styrene for making clings

Copy the patterns and enlarge them if desired. Tape the pattern to your work surface and then tape the styrene over it so the two layers don't move. Practice making even lines with your leading color, keeping the tip of the writer bottle off the plastic slightly and moving your entire arm to make more graceful, smooth lines.

Trace the outlines of each area carefully with the leading color (black or gold), allow to dry 1 to 2 hours. Fill in the various color areas as indicated on the pattern, then allow to dry completely according to the instructions on the paint bottle.

Pattern 1: Ra

Pattern 2: Sekhmet

"BEADED" NATHOR STATUE

I love the look of the beaded fruits often seen in holiday garlands and decorative accents. They look so opulent, like jewels from the earth, or the first frost of autumn. I feel it highlights their bounty and richness to decorate them so, and I wanted to give that feeling of wealth and abundance to a goddess image in the same way.

YOU'LL NEED:

A cookie sheet with raised sides
Newspapers
Small Nathor statue or other stylized goddess image
Small paper plate (or equivalent)
Tacky craft glue
½-inch flat and #1 round paint brushes
Small container of water (like a yogurt cup)
2 ounces of extra-small glass microbeads in your choice of color

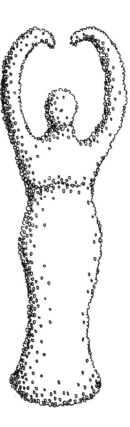

Beaded Statue

Lay the newspapers inside the edges of the cookie sheet to protect it from the glue (the edges will prevent the microbeads from rolling all over the place so they're not wasted and don't make a mess). Examine the statue and remove any loose paint or gilding that could flake off after you add the microbeads. On the small paper plate, pour a few drops of glue and mix a tiny bit of water into it with the ½-inch paint brush to thin the glue. Do not make the glue watery!

Lay the statue on its side and brush a light layer of glue over one side of it. Wipe up any glue drips and allow it to dry for about a minute or until it becomes thick and tacky but not dried out. The idea is to create a thin layer of glue that will not drip off the sides but is wet enough to hold the microbeads in place.

Sprinkle the microbeads over the statue until you have an even coat with no holes in it. Allow to dry completely, then turn the statue over and repeat. When the statue is completely dry and can be handled, allow any loose beads to fall away onto the cookie sheet and examine the statue for "bald" spots. Use the #1 round paint brush if necessary to touch up any areas with glue, adding more beads and allowing to dry completely before handling.

EMBELLISHED JARS AND BOTTLES

Most of us magpie types have stashed away neat bottles that aren't quite altar quality, but we just can't bear to toss them in the recycle bin either. What's the solution? Decorate them! Decorated bottles with a stopper make good storage containers for stick incense, and embellished jars can hold your ritual salt, powder incense, seawater, or anything else you like. They also make great gifts, and this is an ideal project for a group.

YOU'LL NEED:

Interesting jar or bottle (I used a Pom juice bottle)
Design Master 24kt Pure Gold spray paint
Masking tape or painter's blue fine line tape
Craft knife
Krylon Short Cuts craft spray paint in red pepper
Craft glue and small paintbrush (such as #6 round or ¼-inch flat)
Provo Craft Micro Beedz in red, orange and rose
Small dish or cup
Scrap of fabric about 12-inch square
Provo Craft Microfine Sparklerz Glitter in scarlet
Clear coat spray

Spray the top of the bottle with gold, allow to dry completely. Mask off any areas you don't want red and spray the rest of the bottle with the red craft paint. Allow to dry completely. Carefully remove the tape.

Where the red meets the gold, paint a line of glue, using just enough to wet the surface but not so much that it drips. Blend the three colors of Micro Beedz together and lay the fabric scrap on your work area so you can collect what doesn't stick to the glue. Sprinkle the beads over the glue evenly and allow to dry completely. Brush very light, random sweeps of glue over the other surfaces of the bottle and sprinkle with the fine glitter. Allow to dry completely. Protect your finished project with the clear spray finish.

MOSAIC ALTAR VASE

Mosaics were very popular in ancient Greece and Rome, decorating the floors of all kinds of buildings, both public and private. It's fun to lay all the tiles in place and make your own colorful designs, whether they be wild abstract waves of color, or meticulous and realistic images. This project also includes meaningful charms and will add a whimsical and opulent touch to your altar.

Large glass vase or candle holder

Glass cleaner and paper towels

Folded soft towel

Assorted clear glass mosaic shapes

Large tarnish-proof metal charms and old jewelry pieces

Glue gun (if the vase) or clear two-part epoxy (if the candle holder)

Piece of card and toothpicks (if mixing epoxy)

Clean the glass before starting to remove any dust, price tags, and so on. Lay the glass on the folded towel to make working with the lumpy project easier. Select your pieces in advance if possible, laying them on the surface of the glass to check their fit—wide pieces don't lay on a curved surface very well.

Mix the epoxy if using that technique for the candle holder (glue from a glue gun won't hold up under the heat from a candle). Glue each mosaic piece on the glass, laying them in place any way you like.

CONCRETE FOUR DIRECTIONS MINILITHS

If you have an outside ritual circle as I do, you probably need a way to mark the four cardinal directions. In Europe, huge stone megaliths mark the directions and the seasons, so making and setting up your own "miniliths" echoes this ancient practice while including your own creative energies or those of your ritual group.

YOU'LL NEED:

3, 50-pound bags of easy-mix cement or concrete (*not* instant post-setting mix)

Bucket or wheelbarrow

Trowel or shovel or hoe

4, 12-inch lengths of construction reinforcing metal ("rebar")

4 plastic wallpaper paste trays

Assorted mosaic tiles, broken pottery, seashells, etc.

Wet sponge

Medium-stiff bristle cleaning brush

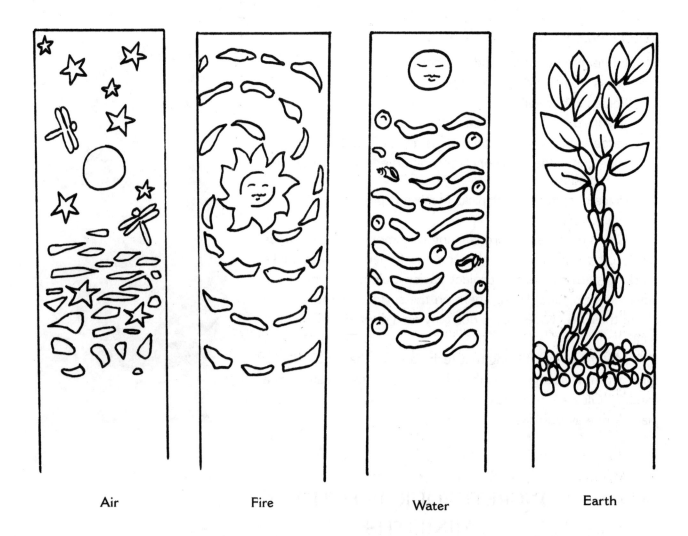

Air   Fire   Water   Earth

In a shady area, mix up the cement in the bucket or wheelbarrow, one bag at a time, according to the bag's instructions. Use any garden tool that works best for you. The cement should neither be overly dry and crumbly nor soupy wet. Pour the cement mixture into the wallpaper trays, then push a piece of rebar into the center of each to strengthen the finished minilith.

Working quickly, and following the designs laid out here, gently and evenly press your mosaic tiles into the surface of the wet cement, wiggling each one into place as needed so that they're seated well and even with each other (as best you can). Depending on the temperature and humidity, you have between 10 and 20 minutes to work on the tiles before the cement becomes too firm. If you're in the sun, you will have even less time, so do this project in the shade if at all possible.

When the cement has cured for a minimum of several hours, go back and use the scrubber to remove any cement residue that is coating your mosaic tiles. Rinse, check your finished mosaic, and scrub again if necessary until all the tiles are clean. Allow the miniliths to cure for at least another 24 hours (longer is better) before attempting to remove them from their molds. Once removed, bury the bottom portion of each one so that your monuments stand upright around your circle.

RESOURCES

Dick Blick
P.O. Box 1267
Galesburg, IL 61402
(800) 828-4548; www.dickblick.com

In the art supply business since 1911, this is your one-stop shop for all manner of fine art and craft supplies. They carry Armour Etch, Pebeo Arti' Stick Window Colors, glass paints, and other glass art supplies.

Diamond Tech
5600 Airport Boulevard, Suite C
Tampa, FL 33634
(800) 937-9593; www.diamondtechcrafts.com

Manufacturer of different kinds of glass and ceramic mosaic supplies, as well as materials and tools for glass bead making and stained glass.

La De Da Designs
7987 Pecue Lane, Suite 1
Baton Rouge, LA 70809
(225) 755-8899; www.ladeda.com

Whimsical source for micro beads, pebbles, bead and glitter mixes, adhesives, and more for embellishing your painted bottles and a myriad of other projects. They also have stacking storage containers for your micro beads and other small, loose materials.

Mosaic Art Supply
743 Edgewood Avenue
Atlanta, GA 30307; www.mosaicartsupply.com

This supplier offers wild mosaic materials not seen elsewhere, such as Italian marble tiles, polished gemstones, Italian glass millefiori circles, metallic glass, and much more. They also carry clear mosaic adhesive for doing glass vases and candleholders.

Mosaic Basics
1856 Chrysler Drive NE
Atlanta, GA 30345
(404) 248-9098; www.mosaicbasics.com

Excellent selection of mosaic tiles and supplies, especially unusual shapes and harder to find mosaic tiles such as glass shapes, shaped ceramic tiles, and faux vintage china pieces.

Mosaic Mercantile
P.O. Box 78206
San Francisco, CA 94107
(877) 9-MOSAIC [966-7242]; www.mosaicmercantile.com

Informative website with free project instructions and a photo gallery of some amazing mosaic designs. A full line of tiles, tools, adhesives, and grouts for the mosaic enthusiast.

Sunshine Discount Crafts
P.O. Box 301
Largo, FL 33779
(800) 729-2878; www.sunshinecrafts.com

Serving professional crafters since 1980, this company has the full line of DecoArt Liquid Rainbow transparent paints as well as themed sets and tips on how to use them. Also carries many other types of craft supplies.

Viking Woodcrafts
1317 8th Street SE
Waseca, MN 56093
(800) 328-0116; www.vikingwoodcrafts.com

Better known for their selection of wooden items and supplies for decorative painting, Viking also carries the complete selection of DecoArt Liquid Rainbow transparent paints.

7

Metal

For some reason metal crafts haven't enjoyed much of a following, and I'm curious as to why this might be. Do people think that they're difficult to do, or the materials are hard to work with, or that special equipment is needed? None of these myths is true, and I find metal crafts just as easy as many other craft techniques. In some cases, it's even easier—to make soap or candles you need special supplies and molds in which to pour hot liquids. Paper making is very time consuming and also needs special screens, yet that's a popular craft, too. There are magazines and television shows devoted to woodworking—now there's a hobby that requires special equipment. Perhaps it's seen as a "men's" material, or "too industrial" and since many crafters are women, they don't think it is something they can work with at the kitchen table.

Whatever the excuses may be, toss them out as poppycock and have fun making beautiful projects with copper foil, painted tin, bent wire, gold leaf, and more. There are thousands of techniques and materials for metal crafts, and this ancient art has been used for millennia to honor the Old Ones in many cultures.

Gold is one of the most recognizable forms of treasure, both ancient and modern. People have lived and died over it, toiled and wondered at this rare eternal metal that never tarnishes and shines like a tiny bit of the sun has fallen to earth. Silver is also highly regarded by both today's crafters and by the ancients. In fact, silver was more valuable than gold in ancient Egypt because it was so rare, and Tutankhamun had a carefully tooled silver pomegranate within the treasures of his tomb. Today, silver is most identified with the moon because of its silvery shimmer that can tarnish as the moon grows dark each month.

Copper has long been used both for decoration and utilitarian purposes in cultures where the mineral occurs naturally. To the Wiccan, copper represents the element of Earth, and as such is used to form ritual patens for the altar or pentacle jewelry. Other more common metals, such as tin, pewter, and alloys, have long been used in the same ways as copper, to form decorative and useful items. Punched tin makes durable and lovely candle lanterns and door panels. Lead-free pewter is a popular way of making inexpensive silver-like jewelry with an excellent amount of detail. And wire jewelry just keeps growing in popularity—even some Hollywood stars have taken pride in making their own jewelry!

To work with metal you need very few tools and even fewer special techniques. Most metal crafts simply involve bending it into various shapes. Even punched holes are ridiculously easy to make with a board, a nail, and a hammer. It doesn't take much to transfer a pattern to a pre-made box and make a decorative punched design, or to bend a bit of wire with some smooth-jaw pliers. Gold leaf requires some finesse to work with, but all you need are a draft-free table, a paint brush, and a bit of soft cloth.

This chapter offers a wide variety of metal crafts, from whisper-thin gold leaf to heavy tin, bent copper wire to crocheted craft wire. Crafters can try all kinds of projects even if you've never done metal crafts before. You may find there's nothing mysterious about working with metal at all. In fact, it might turn out to be your new favorite craft if given the chance!

"BROOM PARKING ONLY"
RUSTY TIN SIGN

Whether you hang it in front of your usual parking spot or by the front door, this simple-to-paint sign will bring a smile to all who see it. Using the DecoArt Metal Paints and sealer allows you to hang the sign outside. Feel free to change the colors of the letters if you prefer a different look, and scale the pattern up or down if you want a different size—just adjust the width of the flat brush if you change the size of the pattern.

YOU'LL NEED:

    4½-inch × 6½-inch rusted tin sign blank
    Newspaper
    Americana Matte Spray Sealer
    Carbon paper
    Pencil or stylus
    DecoArt No-Prep Metal Paint in:
        deep purple
        bright white

cornflower blue

sunlight yellow

burnt sienna

coal black

Brushes: 1 inch flat, #1 script liner, #2 round, #00 round

Paper plate or paint palette

Water cup for brushes

Paper towels

About 1 foot of small brass chain

Wire cutters

Needle-nose pliers

2 large brass jump rings (make sure they fit through the sign's
    holes)

Begin by brushing away any loose rust residue from the metal sign. Lay down newspapers (outside if possible) and spray a light, even coat of the matte sealer over the sign. Allow to dry completely.

Copy the pattern onto the tin sign using the carbon paper and pencil or stylus. Begin by working the larger letters of BROOM with the ½-inch flat brush, using deep purple. Paint the other words below with cornflower blue using the #2 round brush.

On the paper plate or palette, mix a drop each of sunlight yellow and burnt sienna to make a straw brown color. With the ¹/₂-inch flat brush, fill in the bristle area of the broom. Use straight burnt sienna to paint the handle with the #2 round brush.

When the word BROOM is dry, outline all the letters with the script liner brush using bright white. When the broom is dry, paint the basic shape of the bluebird on the top of the handle with cornflower blue using the #2 round brush. With the script liner, paint individual straws in sunlight yellow and burnt sienna over the basic shape of the broom bristles you filled in earlier. Also use the same brush with sunlight yellow to paint a very thin highlight on the handle of the broom and the bird's beak and legs.

With the #00 round brush, using coal black, paint the band around the middle of the broom, dot the bird's eye, paint a thin shadow line on the right side of the broom handle, and paint a shadow under the broom's bristles to suggest the ground. Also use the script liner to paint a coal black shadow on the underside surfaces of all letters and the bird. Allow the entire design to dry completely and spray again with matte sealer.

Cut the chain to length if necessary. If the type of chain will allow it, use the needle-nose pliers to open links and attach them through the predrilled holes of the sign; otherwise use the two jump rings to attach the chain to the sign.

PUNCHED TIN TREASURE BOX

This project couldn't be simpler—take a tin container and punch some holes in it. Well, I admit that it is a bit more artistic than that, but the simple process, no matter how complicated the design, remains the same. The star design and the project are inspired by antique punched tin pie safes, used as storage to keep the pests out while allowing air to circulate. Depending on its size and shape, you could use your box for potpourri, tarot cards, ritual jewelry, or a special altar cloth. If you use it for potpourri, leave off the lining fabric so the fragrance can escape through the holes.

YOU'LL NEED:

Plain tin box with lid, or one that can be painted
Carbon paper
Masking tape
Pencil
Piece of soft pine wood to fit the inside of the box lid
Hammer
Small nails, like smooth finishing nails

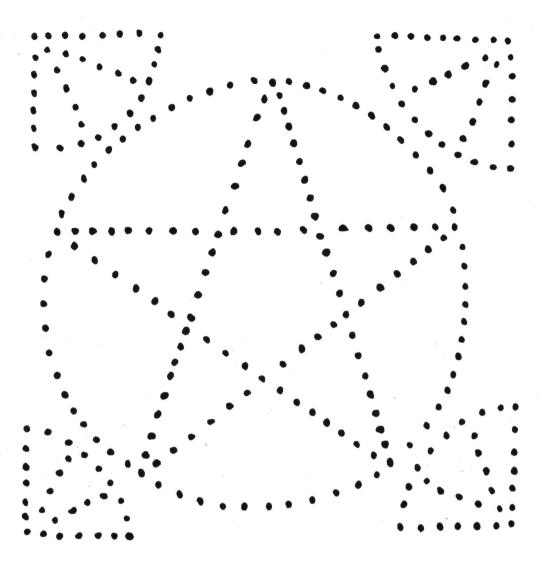

Velvet or other lining fabric (optional)
Scissors (optional)
Tacky craft glue (optional)

Tape the carbon paper and pattern to the lid (you may need to re-size the pattern or find a new one if your box is a different shape). Trace the design firmly with the pencil to transfer it to the lid. Remove the pattern and carbon paper.

Make sure the piece of wood is thicker than the lid—use a folded hand towel underneath to make it thicker if necessary. Lay the lid over the wood and use the nail and hammer to punch holes completely through the lid. Space the holes about ⅛-inch apart.

When the design is complete, you can glue the lining fabric in the lid if desired. Cut the fabric about 2 inches larger than the inside of your lid and fold under all edges 1 inch. Glue these edges under, either before fitting it inside the lid or as you glue the fabric to the lid. Avoid using glue too close to the punched holes; it could ooze through and mar your design.

PUNCHED METAL CANDLE HOLDER

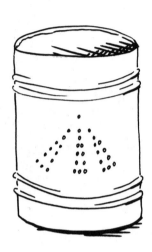

If you've made the punched tin box project, this one will be a snap, too. Instead of a block of wood, however, you will use ice to keep the round shape of the can intact. Imagine making lots of these with your group to line a walkway with candlelight! This is a classic Boy or Girl Scout project, definitely an oldie but a goodie.

YOU'LL NEED:

Clean soup can with the label and top lid removed
China marker pencil
Small towel, folded
Hammer
Small nails, like smooth finishing nails
Paint or other decorations and glue (optional)
Tealight or votive candle

Draw your own design on the side of the can—don't worry about being overly artistic, even simple spirals or star shapes will look great. Fill the soup can with water and place upright in the freezer until completely frozen.

Use the towel as a cradle to help hold the can still as you work. Use the nails to punch holes completely through the metal of the can. When the design is finished, wipe away any remaining pencil marks and paint or decorate the can if desired. Place a lit candle inside and enjoy as darkness falls.

EMBOSSED COPPER FOIL PENTACLE

This interesting project uses a pre-made wooden round with two types of copper for extra effect. Copper wire underneath copper foil adds double the element of Earth to your altar.

YOU'LL NEED:

5-inch × 5-inch wooden round plaque
Fine tip marker or pencil
Metalworks copper coiling rods, thin
Ruler

Diagonal pliers
Needle-nose pliers
Hammer
Craft glue or epoxy (optional)
Copper tooling foil
Utility scissors
Burnisher
4½-inch circle of black felt
Craft glue

Mark the five points of the pentacle on the wooden circle so that they're about ¼ inch in from the edges, then make another mark ¼ inch in from that (see pattern). Cut the copper rods into 5, 3¾-inch lengths. Bend over the ends about ¼ inch at a 90-degree angle so that the ends will fit into the holes. Check the fit of each rod—one end is on the outer mark and the other end is on the inner mark. Lay the rods so that they form the "over/under" pattern of a pentagram and tap the ends into the marks with the hammer. This might take a little persuasion, such as using the pliers to hold the rod as you tap in one end. When the ends are in place, tap on each rod to bend it slightly and help it rest properly over and under its neighbors. If the rods have trouble staying in their holes, use a dot of glue to keep them in place and tap firmly with a hammer.

Cut an 8-inch circle of the copper foil. Center it over the wire pentagram and fold the edges under the bottom. Carefully burnish the foil so that it fits tightly and smoothly over the wire to reveal the pentacle shape. Continue burnishing outward from the center, working the edges of the wooden circle and finishing with the bottom edge. Burnish down any folds that form along the sides of the circle and make the bottom edge nice and crisp.

Center the circle of black felt on the back of the pentacle and glue in place. Wipe any fingerprints off the copper top and spray with clear coat so that it will stay bright copper.

GOLD LEAFED COPPER YULE ORNAMENTS

Shimmering tones of the season make these tree ornaments really special. A golden sun and the sacred mistletoe harvest are rendered in copper foil and gold leaf. It's easier than it looks!

YOU'LL NEED:

Medium copper foil
Scissors
Flat faced needle-nose pliers
Gold leafing kit (gold leaf, sizing, satin coat, brushes, cheesecloth)
Pointed or small ball point stylus
Old mousepad or stack of paper
Ice pick or a hammer and small nail

For each ornament, cut a small square of copper foil (about 2½ inches) with the scissors. Carefully bend over the edges with the pliers and flatten them so they are smooth and safe (don't use pliers with a textured surface or it will mar the foil).

Lay the foil on the mousepad or paper and then lay the pattern on top of the foil square. Use the stylus to trace the pattern, pressing firmly so that it makes grooves in the foil.

Brush the design areas with a light amount of sizing so that it doesn't puddle much in the grooves. Use a freedom brushstroke to cover the major design elements, letting the sizing go outside the areas a bit. When the sizing is completely clear (about 10 minutes depending on the humidity that day), tear off a 3-inch piece of gold leaf and carefully lay it over the ornament. Press the gold into the grooves in the foil with a piece of fabric until the design is even and the gold leaf is pressed fully into it.

Use a paintbrush to sweep away all excess gold so that only the sizing is covered. Don't worry about small breaks in the gold, we're going for a rustic look for these ornaments and the pretty copper will show through beautifully. When all excess gold has been removed, gently brush the satin coat over the entire ornament and allow to dry completely (about 1–2 hours). When dry, use the ice pick or hammer and nail to make a hanging hole in the top corner.

WIRE LABYRINTH PATH PENDANT

Rather than a labyrinth itself, this free-form shape actually represents the path taken within a labyrinth. It looks complicated, but it's very easy as long as you carefully follow the photo. Because of how it's constructed, it can be somewhat delicate and become unbent if it snags on something, so I recommend wearing it only on special occasions (or bring some pliers with you). If you don't make every bend perfect, don't worry about it—as long as it ends up about 1-inch square, you did it right. Don't make it too large, however, or the last several bends that terminate with the hanging loop will be too flimsy to support the rest of the shape.

YOU'LL NEED:

    About 12 inches of 20-gauge copper wire
    Wire cutters
    Small round-nose pliers
    Flat needle-nose pliers with smooth jaws
    Clear spray sealer (optional, to help prevent copper
        from tarnishing)

Begin in the center by making a small loop in the end of the wire with the round-nose pliers. Build this loop by carefully bending the wire around the pliers (don't move the pliers, move the wire), repositioning the pliers as needed to continue the spiral about 2½ times around. Alternately, hold the forming spiral in the jaws of the flat pliers if that technique works better for you.

With the flat pliers, hold the wire about ⅛ inch away from your spiral and bend the wire at a 90-degree angle as shown in the diagram, pressing the wire against the edge of the pliers for a sharp corner. Make sure the bends are on the same plane as the original spiral for a flat finished shape. Move the pliers and continue bending as shown.

Make the last bend up away from the center and leave about 1 inch of wire. To form the wrapped loop, make a large loop with the round pliers about ⅜ inch up from the last bend. Hold the loop tightly with the round pliers in your left hand (if right-handed) and use the flat pliers to wrap the end of the wire around the base of the loop as shown. Trim if necessary and finish the wrap by pressing the cut end flat against the core wire with the pliers.

CROCHETED WIRE FAERIE CIRCLET

This delicate circlet is inspired by the golden circlet of Khnumyet, a princess of ancient Egypt in the Twelfth Dynasty. Wire crochet blends two fun crafts, crochet and wirework, and it's much easier than it looks. If you're new to the idea, don't be intimidated—give it a try!

YOU'LL NEED:

> 1 spool 26-gauge tinned copper wire
> Wire cutters or heavy scissors
> Assorted flower and leaf-pressed glass beads (about 100)
> Size J crochet hook

Thread all the beads onto the wire before starting. Following basic crochet techniques found in chapter 3, "Yarn," make a chain slightly larger than your head circumference where the circlet will rest. Slip stitch in the beginning end of the chain, slide a bead up to your hook, and single crochet in the next chain stitch. Work two more single crochet stitches, then add another bead.

Keep working single crochet stitches, adding a bead every third stitch. The piece is worked in a spiral of four rows. When you reach the end of the fourth row, clip the wire and weave it down to where the other wire tail comes out. Carefully clip the ends to about ¼-inch long, then wrap them around the first chain stitch until the ends are concealed so they don't catch in the wearer's hair.

RESOURCES

Craft Supplies Online
P.O. Box 4221
Shawnee Mission, KS 66204
(800) 999-9513; www.craft-supplies-online.com

Among other offerings, this company has a small but interesting selection of metal craft supplies, including tooling foils, tin shapes, and two sizes of pre-cut copper circles that would make great altar patens.

Island Blue Art Supply Centre
905 Fort Street
Victoria, B.C.
Canada V8V-3K3
(800) 661-3332; www.islandblue.com

Along with a full catalog of other art materials, this Canadian company offers the wire rods and sheet foil used in the copper pentacle project.

Viking Woodcrafts
1317 8th Street SE
Waseca, MN 56093
(800) 328-0116; www.vikingwoodcrafts.com

Although their main product line is wood as their name suggests, Viking also has metal shapes to paint on such as the blank for the "Broom Parking Only" Rusty Tin Sign. Books, paints, brushes, tin items, and loads of other craft supplies are available from this reliable company, which has been in business for many years.

WigJig
P.O. Box 5124
Gaithersburg, MD 20882
(800) 579-WIRE [9473]; www.jewelry-tools.com

Manufacturers of craft wire and wire jigs. Their website, called "WigJig University," features more than 1,500 free wire jewelry ideas and how to work wire with the proper tools.

Wood

As a craft material, wood is one of the most versatile and interesting mediums to work with. Each tree is unique in its qualities based on the location where it grew, the climate, the temperature, the amount of shade or sun, and so on. Two trees growing next to each other, in fact, can show quite a lot of variation between them. Keep this in mind as you select the wood products for your projects—look carefully at the grain, notice if the piece has knots, and learn more about what kind of wood is being used.

Look for smooth, even grain in your pre-made items, avoiding knots in pieces that are going to be carved or painted. Knots can contain larger amounts of oils and can cause brown stains when painted over unless special "stain killer" paints are used. Knots are also harder than the rest of the wood, making them an impossible to carve liability when making a delicate woodcut. But of course, knots also add character when worked into a particular design that will simply be varnished or left natural.

Another problem sometimes encountered is wood from endangered trees or trees not harvested in a sustainable or ecologically friendly way. Many commonly used tropical woods such as teak, mahogany, and rosewood are disappearing species, and entire forests are being cut by local peoples in order to both sell the lumber and to graze cattle and grow sun-intensive crops such as coffee.

It's difficult to find wood products that are guaranteed to be 100 percent ecologically responsible! Avoid this dilemma by haunting thrift stores, and reusing items such as wooden tableware. Try to find the origin of the wood you'll be using, but be aware that often the store or manufacturer will not know. Generally, domestic pine is less ecologically harmful to use since it grows quickly. In fact, there are many "tree farms" already established so that virgin old-growth pine forests are not usually being denuded.

As mentioned previously, trees show individual natural variation, just like people. It may be a subtle thing when confronted with a forest of seemingly identical trees (or wooden objects at the craft store), but you need to take the time when selecting your blank wood to ensure a smooth, high-quality surface. Also select your tools and materials carefully, looking for excellence of product and reliability from the manufacturer. I prefer to use name-brand paints and tools because I can rest easy that one batch will maintain the quality of the previous batch, and I won't fall victim to any nasty surprises like color variations between paint bottles, or carving tools that don't keep their sharpness.

I think this chapter is especially fun because you can use your own creativity to decorate some of the projects so that they're completely unique to you. Let the items on your personal altar choose the colors in the Crackle Finish Offering Plate. Use the Quilt Hoop Frame Drum as your soul's blank canvas and decorate it however you like. Listen to your own deity speak as you embellish the Devotional Shelf project in their honor.

As you work, remember to use all tools safely and keep your fingers out of harm's way. When working with paint and embellishments, however, don't worry about being too much of a neatnick, and focus on the creative result. In fact, one of my personal mottos is "If you don't get paint on your hands, you're not doing it right."

CRACKLE FINISH OFFERING PLATE

A nice touch on your altar is a special decorated plate that's used to offer food, flowers, and other gifts to your deity. You can use either a new wooden plate blank for this project or a thrift store find, and the crackle paint will give it the patina of centuries of sacred offerings.

YOU'LL NEED:

Wooden plate
100-grit sandpaper and scrap of cloth (if necessary)
Two contrasting colors of acrylic craft paint (I used gold and
    forest green)
½ inch or ¾ inch flat paint brush
Delta crackle medium
Gloss clear spray sealer

If you've selected a thrift store plate, sand off any varnish, paint, or other previous finish until you're down to the bare wood. Clean away any dust with a lint-free scrap of cloth (such as an old T-shirt).

Completely cover the plate with a heavy coat of acrylic craft paint and allow to dry thoroughly. Following the directions on the bottle of crackle medium, apply an even coat and allow to dry until tacky, 15 to 40 minutes depending on temperature and humidity. Do not allow the medium to dry completely.

Now brush on a light, even coat of the contrasting color using quick, crisscross strokes to ensure an interesting crackle pattern. Don't overwork this top layer of paint or your cracks will smear together or be too small. Allow to dry completely, then coat with clear spray sealer. If you wish the plate to be waterproof, apply a waterproof sealant according to the package instructions. If you need the plate to be food safe, use a water-based food-safe natural sealant.

"PAGAN STANDARD TIME" STENCILED CLOCK

You've probably been to an event that ends up starting at "Pagan Standard Time," also known as "whenever we get around to it." Some of us are even guilty of falling into that odd time zone ourselves, so you'll need this handy clock to help synchronize you with the rest of the Pagan community.

YOU'LL NEED:

Round wooden clock blank
Carbon paper
Acrylic craft paint (dark color like black or brown, or your choice)
#1 paint brush
Gloss clear spray sealer
Battery-powered clock movement and hands set
Picture hanging hardware if not included with set

Re-size the design to fit onto your clock blank if necessary and transfer it to the blank with the carbon paper. Following the lines with fluid, graceful strokes, trace the pattern with the dark paint in order to make it bolder and easier to see. Alternately, paint the wooden blank a light or dark solid color, allow to dry, and use a contrasting color for the clock design. When the paint is completely dry, spray with sealer. Assemble the clock movement according to the directions on the package and add hanging hardware if necessary.

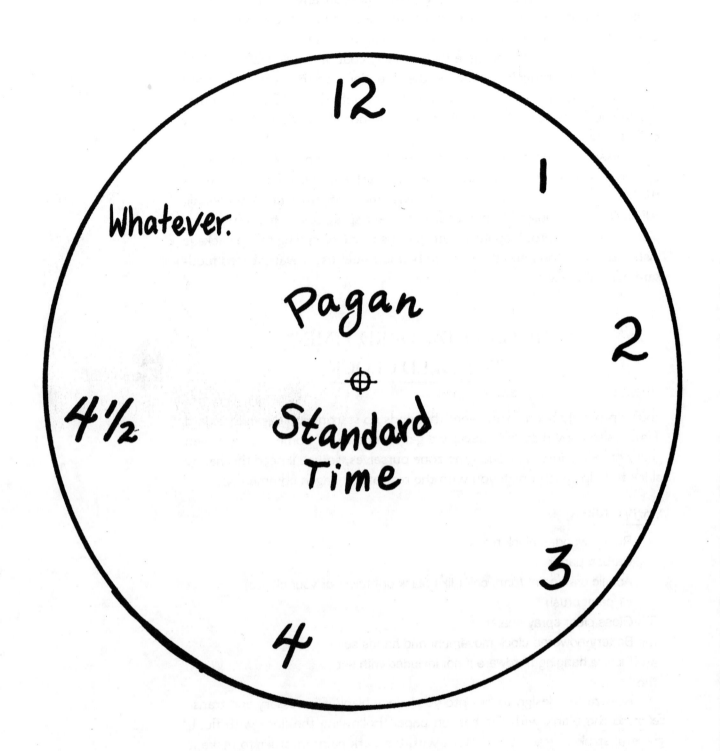

RECLAIMED MARACAS

Many years ago when I was a girl, I got a couple of garish tourist maracas that a relative brought home from Mexico. They got shuffled around for a while because they were so darn ugly, but because they were made from gourds, they had a good sound so I didn't want to throw them away. One Saturday afternoon I got the idea to give them a makeover, and the result is pictured here.

YOU'LL NEED:

> Wooden or gourd maracas
> 100- and 200-grit sandpapers
> Soft tack cloth (such as a scrap
>   of old T-shirt)
> Assorted acrylic craft paints
> Assorted hair craft brushes
> Matte spray finish

Use the 100-grit sandpaper to remove the paint from the maracas, then switch to the 200-grit to give them a smooth painting surface (if the handle is separate, as opposed to being a one-piece wooden maraca, it's not necessary to remove the varnish from the handle unless you want to). Remove all dust with the tack cloth. Paint on your own designs as desired, then seal the paint with the matte spray finish to protect your work of art.

EMBELLISHED DEVOTIONAL SHELF

This particular design was developed for a gold leaf Aphrodite statue of mine, but it's easily adapted for whomever you choose to honor and display atop it. Change the color and types of embellishments any way you like for the most meaningful and complimentary effect.

YOU'LL NEED:

> Small pine wall shelf
> Spackle or wood putty (if needed)
> 100-grit sandpaper
> Gesso
> 1-inch wide flat paint brush
> Brown paper bag

Front View

Top View

Turquoise acrylic craft paint (or your choice of color)
Paper decoupage images
Small, fine-tip scissors
Mod Podge decoupage medium
Iridescent flakes
Blue "angel wing" botanical papermaking includes:
    Glue gun
    Assorted plastic "gem" cabochons or glass blobs
    Assorted seashells
    Matte clear spray sealer
Shelf-hanging hardware if not included with shelf

Fill any nail holes or flaws with spackle or wood putty, allow it to dry, then sand the piece flat with 100-grit sandpaper. Paint the entire shelf with gesso, then allow to dry completely. Sand again, dust, then apply a second coat of gesso. Sand the second coat with a scrap of paper bag, then dust. Cover the shelf with a thick, even coat of turquoise acrylic craft paint, allow to dry, then touch up any thin spots or cover with a second coat of paint as needed.

While waiting for the coats to dry, cut out your decoupage images. I used three iris photographs from a catalog because they reminded me of ocean waves—you could use roses or any other image that is appropriate for the deity you wish to place on the completed shelf. When cutting out pictures for decoupage, use the tips of the scissors and rotate the picture, not the scissors. This is also a good time to arrange your elements so you can decide in advance how everything will be laid out when it's time to glue everything down.

Spread an even coat of Mod Podge medium on the top surface of the shelf. Lay your decoupage images down in the center of the shelf, smoothing them into place and adding more decoupage medium as needed so that they lay properly. Some images will wrinkle slightly—gently spread and smooth them as best you can while the medium dries. When the first coat has dried, apply a second coat of Mod Podge over the entire top. Around the edges of the decoupage images, sprinkle the iridescent flakes into the wet medium so that they stick. Allow the top of the shelf to dry completely.

On the shelf support section underneath the top, use the glue gun to attach your seashells firmly. Next, dab a bit of Mod Podge around the edges of this section, making a border about 1 inch wide. Lay a border of the angel wing botanicals right into the decoupage medium. When this is dry, add your plastic and/or glass "gems" on top of the botanical border. Finally, spray the entire shelf with a light coat of clear matte sealer to protect your work and to make it easier to dust.

"WITCH IS IN" PLAQUE

This fun project can be both useful and whimsical! Those "in the know" will get a chuckle, and everyone else will simply assume it's an amusing self-effacing commentary. If you enjoy painting the front of this project, you can use the same techniques to paint "The Witch Is Out" on the back, using a longer string to hang the finished plaque so that you can flip it over depending on your current status.

YOU'LL NEED:

9-inch wide oval "rustic" wood slice craft blank

Carbon paper and a pen or pencil

Drill with ¼-inch bit (if blank has no pre-drilled holes)

Acrylic craft paints in black, silver, white, brown, green, and opaque red

The Crafty Witch

Paper plate or painting pallette

Water container

½-inch flat brush, #2 round brush, #1 script liner brush

Clear varnish or spray sealant

Length of green or brown suede lacing at least 9 inches long

Copy the pattern to the wooden blank by carefully taping on the carbon paper and then the pattern. Trace with a pen or pencil, being careful not to go outside the lines or make any stray marks that won't be covered by paint. Remove the pattern and carbon paper.

Fill in the large color areas, including the green leaves and black hat with silver buckle. When these areas have dried, hold the flat brush like a calligraphy pen (see diagram) to write the words with brown paint. Now load the flat brush with half black and half brown paint, taking a few practice strokes on the plate to check the mixture. With the black to the outside of the hat's edge, add a brown highlight along the top and brim of the hat as shown. Allow to dry.

Continuing to follow the pattern, add white dot highlights to the silver buckle and add the red ladybug. When these areas have dried, add a black outline to all shapes, including around the buckle, and add the ladybug's black details. Allow to dry completely, then varnish or spray on clear sealant. Add the leather hanging string after the sealant is completely dry.

EMBELLISHED MINIATURE SHRINE

The idea for this project comes from ancient Egypt, where holy statues were kept hidden inside golden shrines and tended only by special priests. Another inspiration was knowing that some people may like to keep an altar, but their roommate or workplace isn't necessarily friendly to their choice of deity. A lovely enclosed shrine keeps the mundane world out and opens a little door to the Divine just for you.

YOU'LL NEED:

Unfinished pine dollhouse wardrobe (1-inch scale)

Small hammer and pliers

100-grit sandpaper or coarse emery board

Gesso

Wood filler (optional, only if you want a perfectly smooth surface)

Tack cloth, such as an old T-shirt scrap

Design Master 24kt Pure Gold spray paint

Color images and decoupage medium or carbon paper and
photocopies of the patterns provided here

Acrylic paint

Fine paint brushes

Water cup and paper towel for paintbrushes

Clear spray sealer

Beads, gemstones, any other decorations (optional)

8-inch square of black or gold fabric

Fabric glue

Small statue, picture, or other devotional image

Your wardrobe will probably have a shelf inside, which needs to be removed to make room for your statue or other devotional item. Carefully break it out with the small hammer, using pliers to remove any large pieces you can't tap out with the hammer. If glue or other tiny bits of the shelf are left, it's okay because you will be lining the interior with fabric and they won't show—large pieces will leave noticeable lumps under the fabric, however, and should be removed.

Check the doors to be sure they don't stick. If there's any sticking or a very tight clearance, sand the doors so they open and close freely. You will be painting the edges of the doors, which will add a tiny amount of thickness, so be sure to allow for this adjusting their clearance. Sand the rest of the cabinet to make all surfaces smooth.

Paint the entire cabinet with a layer of gesso, filling in any rough wood grain as needed. Allow to dry completely. Apply more gesso in layers or use wood filler if you want a completely smooth surface—the gold metallic paint will show every tiny flaw. Sand gently to further smooth the wood, then dust well with a tack cloth. Spray on a light, even coat of the gold paint using short, sweeping movements. Allow to dry, lightly touch up any missed spots, allow to dry completely.

Transfer the designs to the front and sides of the cabinet by first laying down a small piece of carbon paper, then the copy of the pattern. Trace the design with a ball-point pen, pressing firmly, then remove the pattern and carbon paper. (Alternately, apply the color images with decoupage medium.) The top is left blank for your own art ideas, or you can leave it plain and place small offerings on this surface when using the shrine. Fill in the color areas of the designs, then trace the outlines carefully with the liner brush in black. Use long, graceful strokes rather than short dabs for a better line. Spray lightly with the clear coat, coating the shrine evenly and completely without drips. Allow to dry completely.

The Crafty Witch

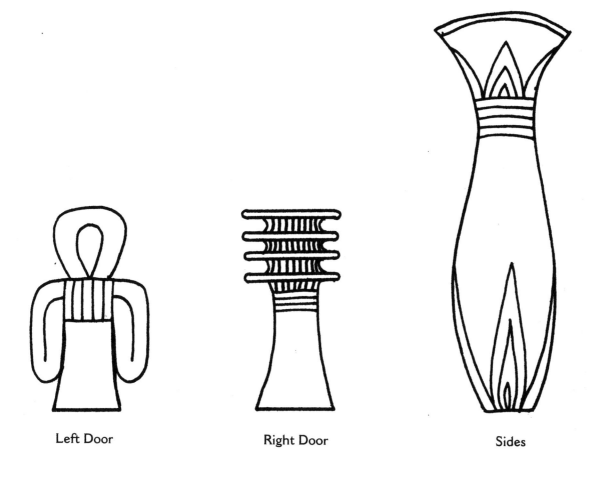

Left Door   **Right Door**   **Sides**

If your devotional image is a light color, use black velvet; if your image is dark, use gold lame. Check the fit of the fabric inside the cabinet by tucking it into the corners and folding the edges under along the front. Be sure the fabric doesn't interfere with the operation of the doors. When you're satisfied with how it fits, spread a thin amount of glue along the top, bottom, and sides, then fit the fabric back in place. Fold the edges under and glue them in place for a finished edge. Allow to dry completely and add your devotional image.

RUSTIC FOLK ART ALBUM COVER

Recently I became quite fascinated with the look of rustic architecture, such as the grand lodges of the national parks that were built in the 1920s and 1930s. During the Depression, rustic folk art often used found or free materials, such as cigarette packs, bottle caps, toothpicks, seashells, and twigs. This unique project celebrates the revival of rustic art and aesthetics, and reminds us of our intimate connection to Mother Earth. I strongly encourage you to go out and find your own twigs for this project rather than just buying them from the craft store!

YOU'LL NEED:

20 to 30 assorted straight twigs, at least 24 inches long, split in half
Pocket or utility knife
Wooden scrapbook cover
200-grit sandpaper
Tack cloths (an old T-shirt works well)
Newspapers
2, 1½-inch paint brushes
Wood stain, "golden oak" or your choice of color
Sharp pruning shears or craft miter box
Tacky craft glue or glue gun
Water-based clear wood varnish

To begin this project you'll need several straight twigs about ¼-inch to ³⁄₈-inch in diameter. Willow twigs work very well as they are straight, easy to split in half, are found growing near water across North America, and come in colors from pale apple green to rich reddish brown. For this project you can gather the twigs any time of year. Split them in half lengthwise, splitting the larger end of the branch with the knife and then carefully pulling the halves apart with your hands, guiding the split with your fingertips. It takes a little practice, but don't worry about doing it perfectly—you're going to be cutting the halves into short lengths to make the album design. If it's spring and the twigs are full of moisture, allow the bark to fall away if it wants to, and let the branches dry before attempting to glue them because the water inside the stems will not allow the glue to bond well.

Prepare the wooden album cover by lightly sanding it so that it's perfectly smooth, then wipe off any dust with one of the tack cloths. Lay down newspapers to

The Crafty Witch

protect your work surface and stain the album cover, carefully following the directions on the container of wood stain. Allow to dry completely before proceeding.

With the largest branches, make a simple frame around the outside edges of the album cover, using perhaps two or three rows of twigs depending on how large you need the space in the center to be. Use only as much glue as you need, clean away any excess glue.

Plan in advance what your album will say-try printing out the letters from your computer using a very simple font so that you can arrange them more easily. Cut the twigs to match the shapes of the paper letters as closely as possible, then arrange and glue the twigs in place. Take your time and line them up carefully. Add other decorations, like twig pentacles or metal charms, as desired. When the letters have all been completed, cut twigs to fit in the corners, building them up with several rows in a decorative way until you're satisfied with it.

If you used tacky craft glue, allow it to dry completely. Varnish the entire album cover according to the directions on the container and allow to dry completely.

QUILT HOOP FRAME DRUM

The original idea for this project appears in the May 1994 issue of *Sunset* magazine and was developed by a teacher at the Quinault Indian Reservation in Washington state (used by permission of Sunset). We made a bunch of these during a workshop at Elderflower Womenspirit Festival one year, and each woman decorated hers uniquely. It was a lot of fun to see the different personalities dance across the drum heads! A special thanks to Leora Forstein for sharing this terrific project during her Elderflower workshop and experimenting with less toxic water-soluble varnishes for me.

YOU'LL NEED:

14-inch to 18-inch diameter wooden quilting hoop with wooden bolt brackets

100-grit sandpaper

Dowel or short branch, approx. 1 inch in diameter and 4 inches to 12 inches long

Small hand saw (such as a coping saw) or band saw

Electric or hand drill

Drill bit the same size as the bolt in the quilt hoop

⅔ yard of heat-shrink Dacron fabric (¾ yard if using an 18-inch hoop)

Household scissors (don't use your best sewing scissors)
Plastic sheeting or plastic trash bag
Craft glue
Household iron
Craft knife such as X-Acto
Clear polyurethane or water-based varnish
1½-inch paint brush
Acrylic craft paints, permanent markers, paint pens, etc.
Clear spray sealer

Sand all surfaces of the wooden hoop to eliminate rough spots and splinters. Now cut one end of the dowel or branch along two sides to form a flattened tab in the middle approximately ¼ inch wide and 1 inch long. Drill a hole through the center of the tab. Check the fit of the handle in the hoop frame by removing the bolt, fitting the handle in the slot, replacing the bolt so that it goes through both halves of the quilt frame and the hole in the handle. Tighten the bolt completely. If the inner hoop falls out too easily, make the tab on the handle narrower until the inner hoop just barely stays put by itself when the bolt is tightened. Take the handle back out and sand

The Crafty Witch

it smooth, then assemble the outer hoop and handle loosely so that it's ready to place over the fabric in the next step.

Cut a piece of Dacron several inches larger than the hoop (it's helpful to lay the outer ring of the hoop on top so you can see how big to make it). This heavy-duty specialty material is used to cover boats and aircraft, so look for it in a marine or aircraft supply store. Put down the plastic sheet or trash bag on your worktable and spread a generous amount of craft glue on the facing sides of the two parts of the hoop (the glue will be on the surfaces that touch each other when the hoop is assembled). Quickly but carefully lay the Dacron over the inner hoop, then press the top half of the hoop over the fabric. Tighten the bolt firmly, then gently tug on the fabric as needed to make a smooth, taut surface without wrinkles. Do not over-stretch the fabric or the frame will warp or break when you shrink the fabric.

Set your iron to about 200 degrees and allow the glue to dry completely as the iron heats up. When the glue is completely dry and cured, gently and quickly sweep the iron over the fabric on both sides to shrink and tighten it. If wrinkles form, sweep the iron over the area until it's smooth. When you're satisfied with the tightness of the drum head, turn the drum over and trim away any excess fabric with the craft knife.

Completely coat all parts of the drum, front and back, with an even, thin coat of clear varnish. Allow to dry, then apply a second coat. Allow to dry completely, then decorate the drum head with the paints and/or markers. Spray with clear sealer to finish.

If you want to make a simple beater for your drum, drill a hole halfway into a 1-inch rubber toy ball, glue a dowel in place, and place a scrap of leather (for a louder, sharper sound) or sheepskin (for a softer sound) over the ball. Tie the leather in place with a bit of embroidery floss.

CORNER HUGGER DRAGON OR GRYPHON

You'll enjoy gazing at these fun decorative accents as they rest over a favorite door, perhaps protecting your treasure? A band saw and scroll saw or jigsaw are the two ideal woodworking tools for this project. The band saw with a wide blade will enable you to make the straight cuts that surround your door frame, and the scroll saw is essential for doing the detailed cutouts that form the dragon or gryphon's outline.

YOU'LL NEED:

24-inch square of ½-inch furniture-grade plywood
Carbon paper and a pen or pencil

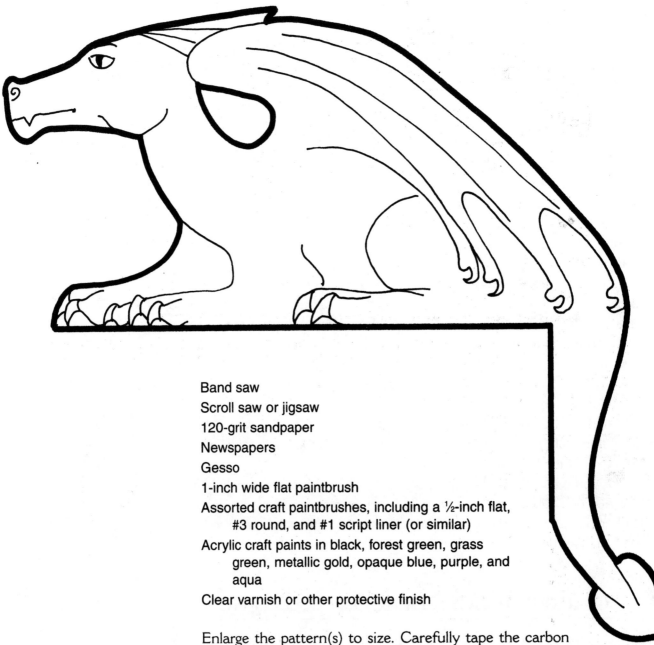

Band saw

Scroll saw or jigsaw

120-grit sandpaper

Newspapers

Gesso

1-inch wide flat paintbrush

Assorted craft paintbrushes, including a ½-inch flat, #3 round, and #1 script liner (or similar)

Acrylic craft paints in black, forest green, grass green, metallic gold, opaque blue, purple, and aqua

Clear varnish or other protective finish

Enlarge the pattern(s) to size. Carefully tape the carbon paper onto one corner of the wood (better side of the wood up if it's one-sided) and then tape the pattern over it, copying the outline of the design onto the wood by tracing it with the pencil or pen, pressing firmly so the carbon paper makes a clean copy. Remove the pattern and carbon paper, setting them aside for later use. Make the two straight cuts with the band saw, and cut out the rest of the design with the scroll saw.

Gently sand the completed wood blank to prepare the surface for painting. Break the corners slightly as well (round off the sharp edges) with the sandpaper and then dust off well. Apply an even coat of gesso to prepare the surface for the craft paint.

The Crafty Witch

When the gesso is dry, sand again gently if there are any uneven areas or drips. Use the carbon paper and pattern again to copy the painting diagram portion onto the prepared wood blank. Working from the bottom layer of color outward, fill in the larger color areas according to the diagram. Now add the next layer(s) of color, gently blending if indicated by using less paint on your brush as you feather out the edges of the color area. When all color areas have been completed, outline the design as shown with black paint using the script liner brush. When all paint is completely dry, coat with clear finish to protect your work.

THREE HARES WOODCUT PRINT

This motif is found first in Asia, but travelled the Silk Road to medieval Britain where it became a popular fertility design in many churches and is often depicted near Green Man panels. This particular design is adapted from a roof boss in the Church of Saints Peter and Paul, Wissembourg, France, circa 1300 CE.

YOU'LL NEED:

    6-inch square or round clear pine board
    Carbon paper and a photocopy of the design
    Walnut Hollow carving tool set
    Craft paint (or printer's ink if you prefer a cleaner image)

3-inch foam brush or foam roller
Paper
Rubber brayer
Soft toothbrush and towels for cleanup

Begin with a perfectly flat board free of knots and imperfections. You should be able to find a board like this either at your local lumber yard or craft store. I carved mine into a pine sign plaque but I've also used simple 1-inch × 8-inch pine planks in the past. Transfer the design onto the wood (see page 132).

When carving, follow the grain of the wood when possible, and take your time to avoid slipping and damaging your design. Begin at the end of a line, such as the rabbit's leg, and gently taper down into a shallow cut with the V-gouge. Use the index finger of your opposite hand to push down gently on top of the gouge and help guide it. If need be, try gently rocking the gouge back and forth to help it through the cut. Take multiple shallow cuts rather than one deep cut as you work. Do not try to take a deep cut with only one hand or you will end up with an out-of-control slice that will ruin your print. Also cut away from you to avoid cutting yourself with the gouges, which are extremely sharp.

Use the flat chisel to slice straight down through the grain of the wood where one line meets another line, such as the rabbits' ears and where the belly cut meets the leg. After the wood is cut vertically, carefully and gently work the V-gouge up to the line and lift up to remove the wood shaving. Use the chisel again if necessary to make a clean cut.

Once the initial cuts are made that outline the entire design, use the small U-gouge to remove the material in the negative space between the rabbits, taking your time and gradually deepening the cuts as you work. When all background areas near the hares have been removed, use the large U-gouge to remove the background around the outside of the design. If you don't want it showing up in your print, it needs to be removed.

With the foam brush or roller, quickly apply a very light layer of acrylic craft paint to the design (if you take too long the paint will begin to dry and make a poor print). Carefully lay your print paper over the paint and use the rubber brayer to firmly press the paper into the paint to make your print. Adjust the amount of paint applied until you're satisfied with the image. Clean the carving before storage by quickly running it under water and scrubbing very gently with a soft toothbrush, then immediately blot dry with towels so that the wood doesn't swell and distort. If you used printer's ink, clean it with the solvent needed and blot dry with paper towels.

RESOURCES

Aircraft Spruce
(877) 4-SPRUCE [477-7823]; www.aircraft-spruce.com

A source for the heat-shrink Dacron fabric used in the frame drum project.

Delta Technical Coatings, Inc.
2550 Pellissier Place
Whittier, CA 90601
(800) 423-4135; www.deltacrafts.com

One of the leading manufacturers of acrylic craft paints as well as numerous other products for woodcrafts, papercrafts, gold leafing, and more.

Design Master
P.O. Box 601
Boulder, CO 80306
(303) 443-5214; www.dmcolor.com

After many years of searching, I've found that this company makes the best metallic gold spray paint. They also make a number of spray colors and finishes for crafters.

Lee Valley Tools Ltd.
P.O. Box 1780
Ogdensburg, NY 13669-6780; www.leevalley.com

Lee Valley is a family-owned business that has been serving users of woodworking and gardening tools since 1978. They have hand tools for the pro as well as the beginning woodworker.

Monfort Associates
50 Haskell Road
Westport, ME 04578
(207) 882-5504; www.gaboats.com

A source for the heat-shrink Dacron fabric used in the frame drum project.

Plaid Enterprises, Inc.
3225 Westech Drive
Norcross, GA 30092
(800) 842-4197; www.plaidonline.com

Since publishing their first macramé instructional book in 1976, Plaid has expanded into one of the world's largest craft materials manufacturers. They make a number of paints, finishes, brushes, stencils, mediums, and more for woodcrafters, some of their lead brands being Mod Podge® decoupage medium, and Apple Barrel® and Folk Art® paints.

Viking Woodcrafts
1317 8th Street SE
Waseca, MN 56093
(800) 328-0116; www.vikingwoodcrafts.com

This is one of the largest suppliers of wooden blanks and supplies for tole painters in the world. Books, paints, brushes, wooden items, and loads of other craft supplies are available from this company, which has been in business for many years.

Walnut Hollow Farm, Inc.
1409 State Road 23
Dodgeville, WI 53533
(800) 950-5101; www.walnuthollow.com

Besides the wood-carving tools used in this chapter, Walnut Hollow makes a wide variety of wooden craft blanks for painting and embellishing.

9

Paper

Far from the days of the ancient Egyptians cutting papyrus by the Nile and pounding strips of it into the first paper, today's paper crafter has an infinite selection of textures, colors, materials, and ideas. Even if you're not into scrapbooking, the explosion of this popular activity has produced an amazing, even bewildering, amount of products for all kinds of paper-based crafts. New acid-free adhesives and stickers, wild punches of any shape and size, blank gift bags and blank cards with envelopes, pre-mixed superfine papier-mache "clay," and lots of other supplies have shown up in major craft chains and smaller independent shops around the world. There's even a half-hour television program devoted to scrapbooking and paper craft techniques!

This chapter encompasses not only the new techniques and ideas, but also explores traditional paper arts that have been nearly forgotten or are only just recently remembered. From early Christian monasteries comes quillwork, the art of scrolling and pinching thin strips of paper into delicate and lacy shapes. It takes a little practice to learn how much to let the coils unwind before gluing the end down, and it does take a lot of patience to put together all the individual elements for a large design like the one in this chapter, but at its center quillwork is a simple craft that you may find quite addictive, especially with the new multicolored paper strips available to today's quiller.

From the Victorian era we have two classic crafts, the recycled Yule card tree ornament and the three-dimensional tole picture. The thrifty Victorian girls and ladies found good uses for the new, colorfully printed greeting cards of the time and made beautiful, decorative items for the home. The projects also bring the static, two-dimensional images to life by forming spheres or layering them to make something new and lovely for the proper home.

No matter whether the materials or project ideas are old or new, paper is definitely one of the most popular and versatile crafts in the world.

FAUX CROSS-STITCH BOOKMARK

Get the look of a hand-stitched bookmark without having to thread a needle! This project is perfect for kids, for those who hate to stitch, or for a quick group project at your next meeting. Have fun using this technique with any charted pattern.

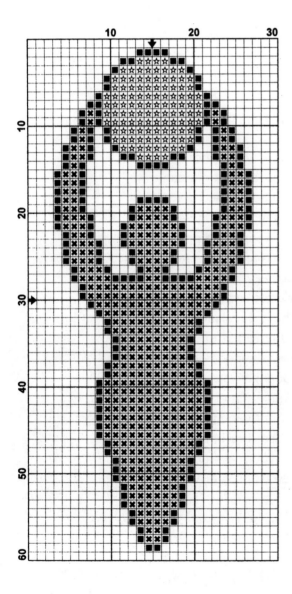

YOU'LL NEED:

14-count perforated paper for cross-stitch
Fine-tip permanent markers in black, blue, purple, and silver
Scissors

Each square equals one "stitch," or the intersection between four holes. If you were to stitch this with thread, you would make an "X" between four holes, and this is where you will place your marker tip. Begin at the top or bottom of the design, putting a dot of color where indicated according to the chart's symbols. The heavy outline is not marked with pen—it's the cutting line for the finished bookmark. Cut out following the dots, do not curve the edges so that you get a realistic cross-stitch look.

Fabric:	Aida 14, White
	24w × 58h Stitches
Size:	14 Count, 1⁵⁄₈w × 4¹⁄₈h in

Floss Used for Full Stitches:

Symbol	Color
■	Black
✖	Blue or your choice
☆	Silver

VICTORIAN RECYCLED
CARD ORNAMENTS

I just love making these because not only do they make use of old holiday cards, it's fun to punch out the circles and arrange them into colorful little balls to decorate for Yule. This is also a period Victorian craft, developed during the big surge of Yuletide popularity that developed in the later nineteenth century, an attribute that scratches my living history itch very nicely. I made a bunch of these to give away to my sewing circle friends and they were a big hit.

YOU'LL NEED:

An assortment of greeting cards
Circle punch, approximately 1-inch
     to 1½-inch across
Tacky craft glue
Scraps of ribbon, trim, or rickrack
Scissors

The size of the circle determines the size of the ornament, with a 1⅛-inch punch producing an ornament about 2½-inches across. The best kind of greeting cards to use have metallic or glittery highlights, or small vignettes of interest like candles, animals, pinecones, stars, and so on. Using the punch upside down so you can see what your circle will contain, punch out numerous decorative circles. You'll need 20 circles per ornament.

Construction

You'll need to fold three segments of the circle up in order to glue the ornament parts together. Orient the design on the circle so that it faces the right way (if it has a picture on it) and decide which way to fold it, either up (A-shaped center) or down (V-shaped center). If you have trouble free-handing the folds, draw a triangle on the back and fold on the lines instead. Or make a paper template for the triangle to make it quicker and easier. You need 10 "up" pieces and 10 "down" pieces to make the ornament.

Begin gluing the top of the ball together by selecting 5 "up" pieces and attaching their flaps together to make a half-globe shape. As you work, press each glue joint together firmly for about 30 seconds until the tacky glue holds securely. Create the bottom part by selecting 5 "down" pieces and gluing them together in the same way to make another half-globe shape.

To create the center ring section of the ornament, alternate 10 up and down pieces to make a circular ring. Match the flaps of the completed bottom section to the center ring and glue in place.

Take a 5-inch long piece of ribbon or trim, fold it in half, and tie an overhand knot in the end to create a loop. Use a pencil or the tip of your scissors to push the top of the loop through the small gap in the top of the ornament and pull it up all the way (if there isn't a gap, use the pencil or scissors tip to create a small hole). Glue the top section to the rest of the ornament to complete the sphere shape.

The Crafty Witch

SUNNY MAY DAY GIFT BAG

Quick and fun to do, you might just find yourself hanging these on your neighbors' doors on May 1 as you ring the bell and run away. If you like to press your own leaves and flowers, they cost almost nothing to make.

YOU'LL NEED:

- Lime green 4½-inch paper bag with handles
- Dried and pressed maidenhair fern sprigs
- Dried and pressed coreopsis blossoms (or yellow flower of your choice)
- Tacky craft glue
- Gold Sanford Uni-Ball Gel Impact pen
- Green Sharpie permanent pen, extra-fine tip
- Pink and yellow botanical "angel wings"

Arrange an L-shaped spray of maidenhair fern sprigs, then glue in place. Select three yellow blossoms and place on top of the ferns until you're happy with the arrangement, then glue in place.

Write "A Merry May Day to You" or similar sentiment in your own best handwriting with the gold gel pen in the area left blank by the fern "L." With the dark green pen follow the gold lines along one side to give them a little shadow and depth.

Select a number of "angel wings" that have a distinct flat edge and opposing fringed edge to them. Overlapping them like scales as you work, and alternating between pink and yellow, glue the wings flat edge facing down and fringed edge sticking up over the edge of the bag. About three wings will fit on the long sides of the bag, and one wing will fit on either side of the fold on each side of the bag.

What a wonderful way to celebrate Yule, by giving a little something to all your circle-mates in a handmade bag. Watch their eyes light up as they ask, "Did you make this for me?"

YOU'LL NEED:

Krylon "Short Cuts" Paint Pen, metallic gold

Scratch paper to practice on

Forest green pinstripe 9-inch paper gift bag with handles

Green and blue assorted handmade papers with gold marbling

Dark green handmade papers

Tacky craft glue

3 skeletal leaves, metallic gold

1 glass or plastic round cabochon in gold, amber, or yellow

Shake up the pen according to the label's instructions, then use the pen's chisel tip to practice some simple calligraphy strokes and to get the ink flowing properly. When you're happy with how your message and letters look, write your sentiment at the top of the bag.

Tear the handmade papers carefully to get a basically straight torn edge with some variations to suggest hills and mountains. Trim to match the width of the bag and layer them, changing their arrangement until you're happy with it. The bag pictured uses dark green nearly halfway up the bag, then a forest green with gold marbling in front, then another layer of dark green, then a final layer in front of dark blue with gold marbling. Glue down each layer, leaving a small unglued area near the top of each layer to add a little depth. Trim if necessary.

Select three gold skeletal leaves and arrange them, stems together, in a sunburst design as shown. Tuck the ends down below the bottom layer of torn paper and glue in place. Add the amber cabochon as shown to depict the rising sun.

GOLDEN PAPERCLAY STAFF HEAD

When our new Egyptian temple hived off from the old one, I had to make a whole new set of these staff heads to represent each of the deities we work with. Using lightweight Paperclay, which is something like an ultra-fine pre-mixed papier-mache, it's easy to achieve these beautiful results even if sculpting isn't "your thing." The staff heads are also detachable for convenient storage and transportation.

YOU'LL NEED:

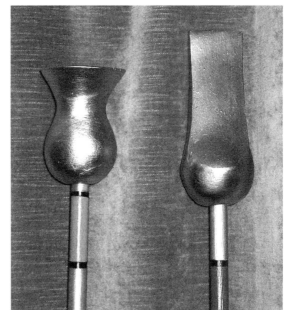

> 12-inch length of ¾-inch diameter wooden
> dowel
> Wax paper
> Masking tape
> Newspaper
> 16-ounce package of Paperclay
> Assorted clay sculpting tools
> Small bowl of water
> 60-grit sandpaper
> 150-grit sandpaper
> Gesso
> ½-inch or ¾-inch flat paint brush
> Design Master 24kt Pure Gold spray paint

Smoothly wrap the end of the wooden dowel with one or two layers of wax paper, securing it with masking tape. The paper should cover about 4 inches of the dowel. Lay down newspaper on your work surface and begin building your basic form with Paperclay around the end of the dowel over the wax paper. Continue working your basic shape with the sculpting tools and your fingers, so that the area around the dowel doesn't become too thin. It should be strong and secure when in use. Make sure that at least 2½-inches or more of the dowel is inside the staff head so that it will sit securely and not topple off.

When the basic form is the shape you want, begin smoothing it with your wet fingertips until it's a smooth, graceful form without cracks or lumps. Allow to dry completely atop the dowel, burying the end in a bucket of sand or stones to hold it upright. The next day check for dryness—if it feels cold to the touch, there's still water deep inside the clay and it should be left for a few more hours.

When it's dry, remove the staff head from the dowel and remove the waxed paper from the dowel. Also remove any paper that might be inside the hole of the staff head. With 60-grit sandpaper, gently sand the form to further shape and refine it, then switch to the 150-grit sandpaper to create a smooth surface all over.

Blow or brush off any remaining dust, then coat the entire staff head with a layer of gesso. When the gesso is completely dry, apply another coat if necessary and allow to dry. The gesso will help further smooth the surface of your sculpture and prevent the gold paint from being absorbed unevenly into the clay. Replace the head on top of the dowel and spray it with the gold spray paint, using even strokes. Don't overspray or you'll get drips along the bottom edges. When the first coat of gold is completely dry, inspect the staff for missed areas and spray again for complete coverage. Allow to dry completely.

POCKET DIVINATION BOX

Here's a cool idea from a very creative friend of mine, Leora Forstein, who also does many other kinds of crafts. It uses a lot of recycled materials and makes a handy gift for those that have everything . . . just theme your decoupage to your friend's tastes and they'll be thrilled by your creativity.

YOU'LL NEED:

Empty mint or cough drop tin with hinged lid
Scissors
Small hole punch
Fine-tip permanent marker
Chipboard, such as from a cereal box
Parchment or colored paper
Black felt
Tacky craft glue
Piece of clear stiff plastic from a package, approx. 4 inch × 5 inch
Small BB, as from a BB gun
Newspaper
Assorted decoupage images, stickers, etc., trimmed to fit and
     pre-arranged
Mod Podge decoupage medium
½-inch paint brush

Make two copies of the basic pattern, sizing it to fit the inside of your tin. Make one copy on the parchment paper, and one on plain scratch paper. Cut out the scratch paper copy and punch out the answer holes. Trace around this pattern and mark the holes on the chipboard three times to make three layers, then cut them out and punch the answer holes, aligning them carefully.

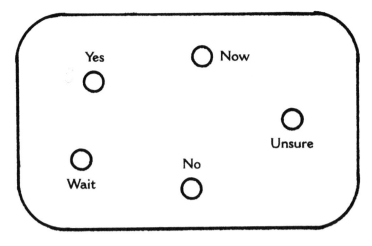

Divination Box Pattern

Use the outline of this pattern to cut out two pieces of felt, but do not punch out any holes. Inside the tin, glue one piece of felt inside the lid, and the other in the bottom. Glue together the three layers of chipboard to make one thick board, aligning the edges and holes carefully. Cut out the parchment paper copy of the pattern and glue it down to the chipboard, carefully aligning the edges and holes and using only a very small amount of glue so that the paper doesn't wrinkle. Glue the completed "sandwich" to the felt in the bottom of the tin and allow to dry completely. All these layers should take up no more than half the thickness of your tin so that the ball has room to roll around the completed project.

Trim the plastic so that it's about a half inch bigger than the inside of the tin all the way around. Round off the corners as well. Using the original pattern or the edge of the tin as a guide, make 2 cuts at each corner up to, but not beyond, the edge of the tin. Crease the edges over sharply, folding them at a 90-degree angle, and slip them inside the tin to form a solid window on top. Check the fit, adding felt at the sides if necessary to fill up any large gaps between the chipboard sandwich and the sides so that the BB doesn't get stuck down the sides when you use the tin. Place the BB in one of the holes to keep it out of the way, then glue the plastic into place, using extra glue if necessary at the corners to seal any small gaps. Allow to dry completely and check the operation of the BB by closing the lid and giving the box a shake.

Lay down some newspaper on your work surface. Brush Mod Podge decoupage medium over the top of the box (and sides if they need decorating). Lay your decoupage images onto the lid, smoothing them gently to avoid puckering and adding a light coat of medium to the backs of any images you wish to place on top of this first layer. When the box is decorated to your satisfaction and the medium has dried, add a final coat of Mod Podge to cover the area that you decorated, giving it a protective finish. Allow to dry completely.

This card is fun to play with but has an important sentiment—your love throughout the turning of the seasons, forever. Around and around it goes, with each sabbat appearing in turn through the peek-a-boo window. Use your own handwriting to make this card—it personalizes your work far more than preprinted text ever could.

YOU'LL NEED:

2 colors of heavyweight scrapbooking paper, 12-inch square pieces

Ruler

Pencil

Drafting compass

Scissors

1½-inch (approx.) circle or square punch or sharp craft knife

Small paper brad

A small scrapbooking sticker for each of the sabbats

Bone folder (optional)

Scrapbooking permanent adhesive

Cut a 6-inch × 12-inch rectangle and 6-inch rectangle from one of the papers to form the outside of the card. Use the compass to draw a 5¾-inch diameter circle in the other color of paper and cut it out to form the spinner wheel. Cut a 5-inch square out of the same color paper as the spinner for the sentiment on the inside of the card.

Following the pattern, punch (or cut) a hole in the 6-inch square and use the point of the compass or the craft knife to make a small brad hole in the middle. Make another hole in the exact center of the spinner wheel. Lay the square on top of the spinner wheel and push the brad through the holes to check the fit of the two parts. Make 8 tiny pencil dots at equal points around the spinner wheel to mark where the stickers will go, centering their positions in the window as the wheel turns. Take the spinner apart and add the stickers, then re-assemble these 2 pieces again.

Fold the large rectangle in half crosswise, using the bone folder if desired to get a crisp fold. Turn it so the fold is away from you and glue the wheel assembly to the top of the card, matching the bottom corners and leaving a gap at the top where the spinner is exposed. Write your sentiment on the 5-inch square and glue it inside the card, centering it carefully.

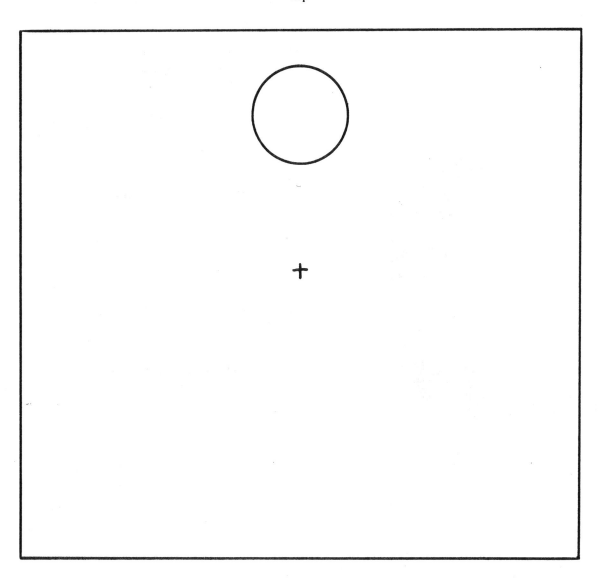

3-D TOLE PICTURES

It seems the clever and frugal Victorians did a lot of paper crafts, and this project heralds from that era of proper young ladies who enjoyed making decorative frivolities in their newly found spare time. The materials used here, however, are thoroughly modern, and the process of deciding where the layers should be requires a lot of visualization skills. The example picture was created by my dear friend Denise Rogers, and I am extremely grateful to her for sharing her project with us.

You'll Need:

    6 copies of a greeting card
    Small picture frame without glass to fit greeting card
    Fine-tip scissors
    Black marker
    Black 1/16-inch thickness craft foam
    Small tube clear bathroom caulk

You will need to study your card carefully to decide where to create the layers, so take your time and imagine that the scene is real. What would be closer, and what would be farther away? Also try to find borders between areas that will make the 3-dimension illusion easier to create, such as a sleeve, or grouping of plants, or some object that blocks part of the picture. Cut on this line so that the cuts are less obvious. Keep one copy of the original picture uncut for reference. Lay out your design in advance so you know where each piece will go.

Touch each cut edge carefully with the black marker so that the white cut edge is covered. Cut a piece of black foam the same size as the small frame and glue your first layer (the one furthest away from you) onto the foam. When this is dry, squeeze small blobs of caulk where the next pieces will go, which builds up a layer of depth. Place the pieces on the caulk, allow to dry. Continue in this way, using the caulk under each layer to give the image depth, until the picture is complete.

Cut several "frames" from the black foam and glue them to the back of the real frame to build it up so that the tole picture fits inside with no exposed edges.

QUILLED DOREEN VALIENTE STAR

The inspiration for this project was a hand-painted Art Deco sculpture that belonged to Doreen Valiente and was used on her personal altar. Using the same colors and layout but completely different materials, this large design will look lovely framed over your own altar. Paper quilling is quite easy, but a project of this size will take some time and patience to complete.

YOU'LL NEED:

2 packages bright white ⅛-inch quilling strips
1 package black ⅛-inch quilling strips
1 package rainbow colors ⅛-inch quilling strips
Quilling tool or large blunt tapestry needle
Scissors
Piece of cardboard
Masking tape
Wax paper
Tacky craft glue
Toothpicks
Large-head pins or T-pins

The design is created from many smaller shapes connected together as seen in the pattern. Each one is formed from a certain length of paper that is coiled and shaped as needed, the longer the paper strip, the larger the shape. Use some of the unneeded purple or orange strips from the rainbow colors pack to practice getting your shapes the right size before starting—it does take some practice to know just how much to let the paper uncoil before gluing down the end to finish the shape. I've also recommended plenty of extra white strips—if you're experienced you may only need one package of white, but it doesn't hurt to have extra, especially when they're so inexpensive.

A quilling tool is highly recommended, but if you can't get one (I don't know why, but some stores have the paper but not the tool), you can make a tool from a large, blunt tapestry needle. Carefully cut or grind the end off the eye of the needle and slip the very end of the paper in the open-ended eye to coil it up.

Top

Black

Yellow

Blue

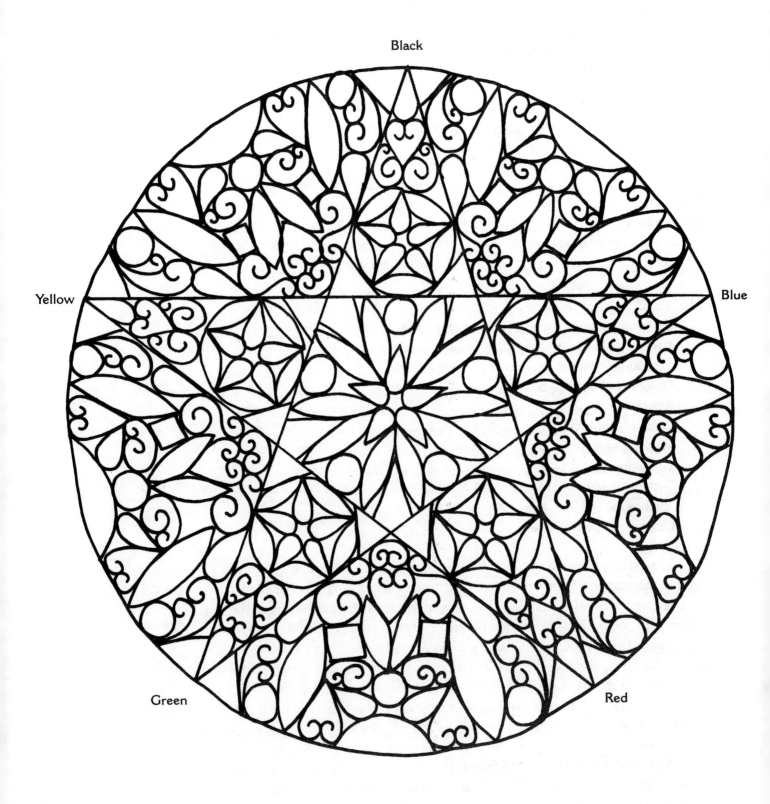

Green

Red

Quilled Doreen Valiente Star Pattern

The shapes used here are teardrops, marquises, loose circles, C-scrolls, hearts, triangles, S-scrolls, squares, plume scrolls, offset marquises, and modified diamonds. Refer to the diagram for each shape, and use the pattern carefully to see which shapes fit into the overall design. If it seems overwhelming, don't worry—each shape is easy to create and you will be building the star one shape at a time from the center out. Take your time, be patient, and your design will start to appear before you know it.

Prepare your work surface by taping a copy of the pattern to the cardboard, and then taping wax paper over the pattern. This will enable you to see the pattern and lay the shapes over it while still being able to remove the design from the wax paper when you're done (use the tip of a pin to tease any stuck pieces loose).

Begin in the center with 5, 6-inch white teardrops, 10, 12-inch white marquises, and 5, 4-inch white loose circles (remember, the inch measurement is how long the strip is before you coil it). Glue the edges of these together as shown on the pattern, using the toothpicks to apply a tiny dot of glue where needed throughout the project. Use the pins as needed to hold the pieces in place as the glue dries. Add 5, 10-inch black modified diamonds as shown. Glue a black strip on all 5 outer edges of the center pentagon.

Now build each star point—you'll need one each in yellow, green, red, blue, and black. Start by connecting 5, 6-inch teardrops into a star, then add 5, 6-inch marquises to create a pentacle. Add the 2, 8-inch triangles in the corners, then the 2, 4-inch C-scrolls, 1, 4-inch heart, and 1, 8-inch teardrop at the tip of the star. Repeat to create all 5 star points, then glue them in place along the sides of the central pentagon. Glue a black strip along the outer edges of each star point.

Continue building the background of the star, which is completely white. From inside the star points to the outer edge and left to right, the shapes you'll need for each section are: 1, 4-inch C-scroll, 2, 8-inch S-scrolls, 1, 4-inch heart, 2, 8-inch teardrops, 2, 8-inch marquises, 2, 8-inch squares, 2, 6-inch plume scrolls, 2, 12-inch marquises, 2, 4-inch C-scrolls, 3, 6-inch loose circles, 2, 6-inch teardrops, 2, 6-inch hearts, 2, 10-inch triangles, and 1, 10-inch offset marquise. Finish the design by gluing a black strip all along the outside edge of the circle.

RESOURCES

Creative Paperclay Company, Inc.
79 Daily Drive, Suite 101
Camarillo, CA 93010
(805) 484-6648; www.paperclay.com

This is the manufacturer of Paperclay, which is made of certified nontoxic and natural ingredients that include volcanic ash, water, and wood pulp. It's biodegradable, lightweight when dry, durable, easy to use, easy to clean up, and easy to find at most craft stores or on the Web.

Dick Blick
P.O. Box 1267
Galesburg, IL 61402
(800) 828-4548; www.dickblick.com

In the art supply business since 1911, this is your one-stop shop for all manner of fine art supplies, papers, drawing and painting media, storage, and everything else you can think of. For the purposes of this chapter in particular, they carry metallic scratch art papers, "angel wing" botanicals, and supplies for making illuminated manuscripts.

Frantic Stamper
186 Ayres Street
Eagle Point, OR 97524
(877) 242-FRAN [3726]; www.franticstamper.com

A huge variety of papercraft and scrapbooking supplies, including Mizuhiki cord, big punches, skeleton leaves, and decorative papers. Be prepared to spend a long time drooling over all the goodies on this website!

Paper Reflections/DMD Industries
2300 S. Old Missouri Road
Springdale, AR 72764
(800) 805-9890; www.dmdind.com

Maker of many handy paper craft items, such as the gift bags used in this chapter, blank greeting cards, paper sacks for embellishing, and more. Paper Reflections takes pride in using recycled materials as well as the assistance of local shelters for the disabled to make their products.

Quilled Creations
P.O. Box 492
Penfield, NY 14526
(877) QUILLED [784-5533]; www.quilledcreations.com

Maker of all kinds of quilling papers, from plain colors to interesting fades, two-sided strips, and more. A complete supplier for this paper craft, and their good customer service is a plus too.

10

From the Garden

Gardening has been a big part of my life. I still remember the roses my grandfather planted at our house in San Francisco, and I would pretend they were a forest for my little plastic animals to prance around in. Later, at our new house in the suburbs, my mother planted a large vegetable garden with corn and beans and chard that we all enjoyed on warm summer nights between bouts of dashing through the sprinklers. Our next-door neighbor had an even bigger vegetable garden, plus the added miracle of mature apricot, apple, and fig trees. We felt like we were growing up in the Garden of Eden as we picked truly ripe foods, still warm from the sunshine.

Now that I live in a rural area, I've been able to re-create a big veggie garden as well as becoming even more familiar with the local native plants. I see the acorns fall that the local Indians used for their staple food. I nod to the artemisia sage that they use in the sweat lodge ceremony. I watch the soaproot grow and know that when fresh you really can use it as soap, and when dry the fibers make a wonderful hair and utility brush.

Our ancestors not only knew the names of all the plant people, they relied on them to survive and for spiritual needs. Flax to make linen cloth, wheat to eat and to weave charms, sticks to make brooms, herbs to flavor, scent, and heal . . . the green people have always been there for us and we honor them with this chapter.

The projects here are both old and new, traditional and innovative, natural and man-made. The classic "Witch's Ladder" usually made with feathers is here created with a series of dried herbs, each one with its own meaning and purpose in the charm. An essential tool for many Witches is the besom, the traditional twig broom that's used to sweep the circle before beginning a ritual. A besom can be purchased, but as you probably know, it's best to make your own tools so that you can put a little of yourself into them.

Among the more "modern" projects, we have Stamped Garden Stakes, which not only mark your garden rows in a practical way, they're created using stamps carved from potatoes. The new paint pens designed for writing on terra cotta are also put to good use on a couple of whimsical and sprightly garden pots, perfect for filling with annuals for your front porch on May Day.

There's a lot of fun techniques and materials in this diverse chapter for you to explore and play with. Make something traditional, or try something new . . . but whatever you do, remember how important the green people are to you.

DRIED HERB CHARM LADDER

As you gather your herbs for this project, hold and smell each one as you think about how they grew, where they came from, how they enjoyed the water and sunshine, then give thanks for their lives before beginning your ladder.

YOU'LL NEED:

> 1 yard of cotton string
> 1 sprig each of 9 different herbs, such as angelica, basil, carnation,
> chamomile, cypress, holly, mint, mistletoe, and rosemary

Use whatever herbs are most meaningful to you, or use the ones suggested here. Angelica wards off evil and removes curses, basil encourages love and friendship, carnation promotes healing, chamomile attracts money, cypress is both protective and grants longevity, holly is strongly protective for the home (especially against natural disasters) as well as promoting good luck, mint draws friendly spirits and protects the home, mistletoe wards against illness, and rosemary is for mental power and overall protection. The sprigs can be fresh or dried—they will dry on the string, so it really doesn't matter which you use.

Bless the cotton string and the herb sprigs, then tie each sprig onto the string very tightly as you focus on its meaning. Start at one end of the string and work your way to the other. Tie a loop in the end of the string and hang in your attic or other hidden place to protect and bless your home.

The Crafty Witch

POTATO STAMPED GARDEN STAKES

If you're like me and have a large vegetable garden, you plant more than one row of each veggie. Store-bought stakes are really expensive, especially when one season out in the sun and rain quickly wears them out. Use the earthy potato to make as many garden stakes as you need, then you can even bury your stamp and grow more potatoes!

YOU'LL NEED:

> Several potatoes
> Sharp paring knife or X-Acto knife
> Utility knife
> Wooden paint stir sticks
> Spray paint (optional)
> Acrylic craft paints
> Paper plate
> Paper towel
> ½-inch flat paint brush
> Permanent marker (optional)

Cut a potato in half to make two stamps. On one half, use the tip of the knife to outline your vegetable shape, keeping it as simple as possible—remember that color will also let people know if it's a carrot or beet or whatever. The shape should also be no wider than the stick, usually about 1 inch. When the outline has been sliced cleanly, cut away the background by slicing sideways toward your veggie shape, the tip of the knife just grazing your shape. Work slowly and carefully, both for safety and so that you don't accidentally take away part of your stamp design. Try not to undercut the edges of the stamp.

With the utility knife, cut away part of the stir stick handle so that the end is roughly pointed. If the stick isn't flat, lay it so that the convex side is up (it's very difficult to stamp down into a concave shape). If this means that the convex side is covered with advertising printing, you may need to spray the stick a solid color first. Cover your painting area with several layers of newspaper, then pour a little of the craft paint onto a paper plate. "Stamp" the potato onto the paper towel to remove any moisture, then use the paint brush to lay a light, even coat of paint onto your stamp. Make a test impression on the newspaper, then brush on a little more paint and stamp the blunt end of your stick. If the stick is very convex, carefully rock the stamp so that a good impression is made. You can also use two different stamps for two colors in the design, such as a green bushy "top" stamp that will work with all of your root crop stamps.

If you want to identify the particular variety in each row, use the permanent marker to write on the stake, either below the stamp or on the back if it's not imprinted with the store logo. For example, you might make six stamped stakes for lettuce which all look the same, then write "Four Seasons" on one, "Simpson Black Seeded" on another, and so on.

DECORATED CLAY POTS

These silly designs are reminiscent of the whimsical kitchenware of the 1950s, where it seemed like everything had a funny face on it. Follow the directions on the paint pens carefully and they're very easy to use. I'm guessing that soon after you try this project, every terra cotta pot you own will have a face or some sort of colorful design!

YOU'LL NEED:

Carbon paper or pencil
Terra cotta pots (ideally new and clean so the paint will adhere well)
Paint markers for drawing on terra cotta
Soil and plants (optional)

Transfer the face design onto the pot with the carbon paper or freehand it with the pencil. Fill in color areas with the appropriate color pen, then use black to draw all the outlines and other features. Allow to dry thoroughly before filling with soil and plants.

The Crafty Witch

CLAPPER STICK

An ancient rhythm instrument of the California Indians, the clapper stick is traditionally made of hollowed elderberry branch. This version is easier to make and produces a much sharper "clack" which is easier to hear in a raucous drum circle or above the noise of a crowd.

YOU'LL NEED:

18-inch length of dried bamboo about 1 to 1½-inches in diameter
150-grit sandpaper (optional)
Paring knife
Small scrap of paper about ¾-inch × 2-inch
Strips of suede or fabric
Beads

Start by sanding the bamboo so that it's perfectly smooth and has no splinters or rough edges. One end should have a joint about 4 or 5 inches from the end—this will be your handle end. Very carefully split the other end of the bamboo with your paring knife to this joint. Bamboo can split further than you intend quickly and unexpectedly, so always hold the bamboo behind the knife blade to avoid an accidental cut. As you approach the joint, slow down and split it carefully so you don't pop the joint open. Another, even simpler option is to use the split rod from an embroidery scroll frame (see photo, left), but the resulting sound isn't as loud.

Fold the scrap of paper in half and slip it down the opening all the way to the joint. This shim will hold the split open slightly as you play it. Test the sound of the clapper by holding the handle section in one hand and hitting the split end against your other hand. It should make a nice "clack" sound. Adjust the paper until it sounds the way you like.

Wrap the handle area behind the paper shim with the leather or fabric. You can either lay one end of the strip on the handle and cover it with successive wraps, or you can start in the middle of the strip and wrap in opposite directions to leave loose ends that are tied together. Secure the end(s) of the strip, and add beads, knotting the end of the strip to hold them in place.

WHEEL OF THE YEAR WREATH

This project was inspired by a very wonderful wreath made by a former circle sister. We used it at a Yule ritual to show the turning of the Wheel, and she must have spent years finding just the right little goodies for that elaborate version. This wreath is more subtle, but you can certainly "witch it up" by adding more obvious symbols to each of the eight sabbat sections. It's designed to be turned to reflect the current sabbat, but of course you can leave it in one favorite position if you prefer.

YOU'LL NEED:

14-inch straw wreath base

Permanent marker

Assorted florals and mini floral picks to represent each sabbat, such as glittered pine boughs, white flowers, daffodils, roses, sunflowers, berries, wheat, apples, mini vegetables, and bare branches (use whatever speaks to you of each holiday)

Miniature bird nest and package of mini speckled eggs

Wired bumble bee and butterfly
Small "primitive" or witch broom
Wire cutters
Glue gun
Large paper clip

Begin by marking the wreath in 8 sections—make a short line, make another line directly opposite the first, then divide these sections in half, then divide in half again so that you have 8 equal sections.

Lay out all your materials on a large table and sort it by sabbat and season. For Yule I used evergreens, red berries that look like they have frost on them, and sparkly gold pine branches. Imbolc uses silver sparkly pine branches, white flowers, flocked greens, and very pale greens. Ostara features a small nest with eggs, more greenery, and sweet pea flowers with tendrils. Beltane bursts forth with larger colorful flowers, darker greenery, beaded strawberries, and a butterfly and bee. A prominent sunflower is the perfect thing for Litha, surrounded by smaller golden daisies and greenery. With Lammas the greenery begins to become more yellowed, and wheat is the main accent here, along with a squash and ear of multicolored corn. This leads into Mabon with harvest-colored leaves, grasses, golden berries, apples, and more squash. Samhain is represented by a small besom surrounded with an apple, squash, autumn leaves, and two very dark green leaves with a mist of frost-like microbeads on them hinting at the winter to come.

Begin heating the glue gun and begin clipping your materials to length. You can do this all at once or as you work each section. Begin at Samhain or Yule (wherever your new year begins) and first lay down the larger background elements such as foliage (these should get extra glue to ensure a secure attachment). Overlap all pieces in the same direction for a seamless look and to help draw the eye around and around the wreath. Don't glue anything in a direction that will look illogical when the wreath is turned and hung differently according to the season. For example, if you place the Ostara bird's nest up on the top edge of the wreath, when it's Mabon it will perpetually look as though the eggs are about to fall to their doom!

Glue each piece down carefully as you work, taking your time and setting each item into the wreath just right. Check before you glue—lay the pieces you want to use down on the wreath first, check where they touch so you know where to apply the glue, and then attach. Avoid attaching elements to each other rather than to the wreath base itself so that they don't come loose later.

When you're finished, remove any glue "spiderwebs" that may have been created by the glue gun. Unbend the paperclip and make a removable hanging hook which will be plunged into the straw. This way you can turn the wreath on each sabbat and re-hang it to reflect the season if you wish.

The Crafty Witch

LEAF DECOUPAGE BOX

Lately I've been seeing more and more flowers and leaves, pressed and dried, being used on the covers of meditation journals, in scrapbooking and other paper crafts, on candles and lampshades . . . everywhere! I thought this would be a fun project that enables you to pick flowers and leaves of importance to you personally and mount them on a little treasure box. You can use magical herbs, pressed flowers from a special bouquet, pretty leaves from a trip, or any botanical meaningful to you that can be pressed very flat and thin.

YOU'LL NEED:

    Scrap newspaper
    Papier-mache lidded box
    Craft paint (optional)
    Flat craft brush, approx. ¾-inch wide
    Assorted leaves and flowers, dried and pressed
    Scissors
    Mod Podge, your choice of satin or gloss finish

Begin by laying down the newspaper on a table to protect the surface. Paint the box before adding the botanicals if desired, allow to dry completely. Cut a circle of paper the same size as the lid of the box and arrange your leaves and flowers on it, trimming them to fit if necessary. When you're satisfied with the arrangement, brush a coat of Mod Podge onto the box lid and transfer the arrangement from the paper. If you have multiple overlapping leaves and flowers, place the items on the bottom first, then add a tiny bit of Mod Podge to the back of each item when you position it so that everything is secured and glued in place.

Repeat these steps for the sides if you choose to decorate them, but fit the lid to the box and mark where the lid overlaps before decorating. Painting the entire side will work fine, but if you add botanicals to the sides where the lid rests it will be too thick to allow the lid to slip over the top (if that's the type of box you have). When the box is decorated the way you want, brush an even coat of Mod Podge over the entire box, inside and out, to give it a clear protective finish.

GOURD DEVOTIONAL BOWL

The dried hard shell gourd is the perfect natural container! Grown to make water dippers, bowls, and carrying containers, gourds have long been used in many cultures. With some caution and patience, they can be easy to work with and a lot of fun, too. The example pictured here is intended for altar offerings and is cut from a small pear-shaped gourd, but you can use any gourd with a bowl-shaped bottom, and any size you like.

YOU'LL NEED:

Hard-shell gourd
Small miter saw
Spoon
100-grit sandpaper
Pencil
X-Acto knife
Emery board (optional)
Acrylic craft paints and brushes (optional)
Food-safe water-based varnish and brush
(optional)

Cut the top off the gourd to create the bowl shape you want. Clean out the inside with the spoon, just like a Halloween pumpkin, and give the seeds to your favorite gardener. Be careful not to breathe the fine dust if possible (it's not toxic, just very dusty). Use a little piece of sandpaper to further clean and smooth the inside of the bowl.

Lightly draw your cut-out design on the outside of the bowl. Very carefully trace it with the X-Acto knife, being careful not to slip and cut yourself. Trace the design over and over, each trace being deeper than the last, carefully plunging the knife deeper as you work to finally cut out the shape. You can also carefully pop it out from the back if you can see that it's cut through and ready to come out. When the shapes have been cut out, smooth them gently with the sandpaper or emery board. Wipe away all excess dust. Paint your gourd if desired, and coat (inside and out) with food-safe varnish if it will be used for food that you intend to eat later.

WOVEN WHEAT PENTACLE

My Elderflower sister Sierra makes these wonderful wheat pieces and she's graciously allowed me to include it here. You can find wheat bundles at many craft stores in the dried floral materials sections.

YOU'LL NEED:

At least 15 stalks of dried wheat

Wall paper soaking tray

1 tablespoon liquid glycerin (optional, makes the wheat more pliable)

12-inch metal ring

1 package natural raffia

Glue gun

Pen or pencil

String or tape measure

Thin cotton crochet thread, straw colored

Scissors

Dried flower fixative (optional)

Sort through wheat stalks, grouping them by 3's. Combine those wheat-heads together that are similar in size and length. Look at the stalks as well to ensure that stalk thickness and color in each grouping is as similar as possible. Discard any misshapen heads or stalks that are too short. You may also need to peel leaves off the stalk. Since you're going to be braiding them, having stalks similar in width and color will make for a better-looking result.

Fill the soaking tub with hot water and add the liquid glycerin, mixing well. Add your wheat to the water, pushing it down every few minutes. As the wheat absorbs water it will settle down and not float so much. The wheat generally needs to soak at least 4 hours—I leave it overnight to ensure full re-hydrating and maximum flexibility. Note that if the wheat is dyed, the soaking will lighten the color.

Prepare your metal circle by wrapping it completely with raffia. Use the hot glue to attach the beginning of the raffia to the ring, and then again at the end of each piece once you've wrapped as far as your piece of raffia will go. Make sure that all metal surfaces are covered—you don't want any shiny stuff showing through! As you add pieces to continue wrapping, overlap the ending and beginning pieces. Wrap the ring surface as evenly and smoothly as possible.

Once the ring has been completely wrapped, mark out 5 equal points with the pen or pencil. These will be the "points" of your pentacle. You can use a tape measure, or you can "eyeball" where the points should be by using string wrapped around the circle in the form of a pentagram. Once it looks right, mark the points with your pencil and remove the string.

When the wheat stems are pliable, and the stalks can bend without breaking, empty the water from the soaking tub and gather your wheat into 5 bundles of 3 heads each. Again, take time to ensure that heads and stems are similar in size, thickness, and color. Taking a bundle of 3 wheat stems and using a long string (at least 12 inches), tie the bundle together tightly just under the wheat heads (as close as you can get under the heads, but still on the stem). If they are tied tightly enough, the wheat heads will "fan" out. Make sure your knots are tight. Do not cut the string!

At the point where the bundle is tied together, glue each one to each mark on the ring. Now use the string to tie the wheat heads to the ring securely. Make sure your string knot and ends are on top of the wheat bundle and not on the underside and in the glue.

Once this is done you can braid the wheat, keeping some tension on it to ensure a straight braid. Wheat is not as pliable as fiber so the braiding requires more of a bending process. You may wish to practice on extra wheat to get the feel for it before starting on your actual piece. Braid the stalks until you run out of stalk and tie off with string. Trim the ends if necessary. Repeat for all 5 points of the pentacle.

The Crafty Witch

Once all of the bundles are attached to the ring and braided, begin to create the star shape. Pick a braid and glue it to the *back* of a point where another wheat head is tied. As you are weaving the star shape, remember that most pentacles have the lines making up the star woven over and under each other where they intersect. Important: make sure you keep tension on the braid to make a clean, straight line while gluing! Once glued, use string to reinforce the attachment by tying it to the ring and over the top of the wheat-heads on the front. Make the final knot in back and secure with a dot of glue. Continue this until you have a completed pentacle.

The final step is to cover the string attaching the wheat to the circle using more raffia. Wrap with raffia until the string is covered using a "criss-cross" wrap. Knot the raffia at the back of the pentacle and set it with a final dab of glue if desired.

Let the pentacle dry on a flat surface away from cats and small hands. Once the wheat has dried, it can be sprayed with dried flower fixative and left to dry again. The fixative is optional, but may help keep the wheat heads from shedding seeds years down the line. Once dry, your wheat pentacle is ready to be hung. If you live in an area that has a wet winter, it's best to keep the pentacle inside since it will mold. The pentacle should last as long as you wish to keep it.

TRADITIONAL BESOM

There are many ways of making a broom, but this style is based on the traditional birch twig besom still made in some parts of Britain. Take care to gather your twigs in the winter only, so that there are no leaves attached and the water is out of the branch while the tree is sleeping—in the fall or spring, the branch will still have enough sap that as the twigs dry they will shrink and your broom will come loose and require re-tying.

Old-style besoms are round, not flat, since flat brooms were invented by the Shakers in the nineteenth century. You can individualize your besom by using colored twine, making a longer or shorter handle, binding the brush with 16-gauge galvanized wire instead of twine as some besom makers now do, drilling a hole in the end of the handle for a cord, or by using different materials that may have more meaning to you personally. Another nice touch, especially if your besom is decorative only, is to add some dried lavender stems or other herbs to the brush.

You'll Need:

Bundle of birch, heather, or scotch broom twigs, gathered in winter, between 18 inches and 30 inches long

Sturdy jute or cotton twine

Scissors

3-foot length of ¾-inch diameter straight branch (traditionally ash) or wooden dowel

Utility knife or sharp woodworking hatchet

Copper or galvanized 1-inch box nails

Hammer

Take a bundle of twigs about 5 inches in diameter and tamp the cut ends together until they're even. Rock the bundle back and forth on your lap to help tighten the twigs together, holding the bundle tightly in your hands as you work. The bundle should lose at least a ½-inch of diameter as it tightens up. When you're satisfied that the bundle is as tight as possible, wrap twine around the bundle two or three times very tightly, about 3 or 4 inches from the butt end, then knot the loose end of the twine to the working end. Continue wrapping the bundle very tightly several times, covering the knot as you wrap. You should have about a dozen wraps on the brush. Cut the twine and tie off securely, then tuck the cut end up into the brush. Wrap the brush again in the same way about 3 or 4 inches down from the first wrapping.

With the knife or hatchet, cut one end of the handle into a point, much like the end of a pencil. You can use sandpaper to refine the point if you wish. Set this point into the very center of your completed brush, then push the parts together very firmly. Lay the besom on the ground and kneel on the brush as you continue to work the handle inside the tightly bound bundle. You may need a partner to help pound the handle into the brush for a good tight fit. When the handle is securely embedded within the brush, drive 3 nails, evenly spaced, through the upper wrappings and into the handle of the besom to attach the brush to the handle.

RESOURCES

Beverly's Crafts & Fabrics
25 Hanger Way
Watsonville, CA 95076
(831) 768-8428; www.save-on-crafts.com

Everything you need for floral crafts and wedding decorations, including wreath forms, silk flowers, faux fruit, holiday picks, glassware, and loads more. A family owned and operated business since 1968, they have 28 stores throughout California.

Richter's Herbs

357 Highway 47
Goodwood, Ontario, L0C 1A0, Canada
(905) 640-6677; www.richters.com

The best source of herbs and dyeplants in the world! They have seeds for just about every kind of medicinal and magical herb you can think of, and many varieties are also available as live plants that they will ship to your door.

Roland's of California

8768 9th Street
Rancho Cucamonga, CA 91730
(909) 982-2601; www.rolandsofcalifornia.com

Enjoy looking through the wide array of botanicals and other floral supplies for making wreaths, arrangements, or other related crafts.

Suchan Wheat

607 North 1050 West
Paul, ID 83347
(208) 438-5745; www.suchanwheat.com

A small family business that has a very nicely packaged selection of many different wheat varieties for weaving, plus a handy gauge for determining the size of the weaving straws.

11

From the Cauldron

When I think of a cauldron, a huge, black, iron pot full of mysterious liquid comes to mind, bubbling and boiling as steam comes up and swirls around, a glowing, crackling fire beneath it. You may not use an iron cauldron over an open fire to make the crafts in this chapter, but when I make candles or soap, working with those mysterious hot liquids reminds me of something that could come out of a bubbling cauldron . . . and who knows, maybe they did a long time ago.

In *Witch Crafts* I discussed candle making materials, supplies, and techniques in a lot of detail. Because I want to introduce as much new material in this book as possible, the candle projects are very simple and only one involves actually melting wax. Whipping the liquid wax, however, is a technique that not many hobbyist candle makers realize is possible, and I thought it would be a fun and interesting project to include that's different from the usual poured candles.

Beeswax is used in this chapter, but not in candles. Many medicinal ointments and salves use a beeswax base to hold the herbs and oils in suspension, making a solid product that is easier to use and store. Beeswax makes an excellent base because it's somewhat soft and softens easily when warm, it mixes well with other ingredients, and it's much more gentle on the human body than petroleum products found in most other commercially made body care products.

Two kinds of soap making are covered here as well, both the easy "melt and pour" method and the cold-process method, which uses a chemical reaction between lye and fat to create finished bars of soap. Anyone can do "melt and pour"; all you need are the soap base, fragrances or other things to be mixed in, and a mold. It's even easier than making candles because there's no wick, leaking molds, wasted excess, double boilers, or messy dipping of tapers.

Cold-process soap, however, is a bit trickier. If you've ever made old-fashioned fudge from scratch, you know that there's a very small window between the "not quite there yet" stage and the "oops . . . too late" stage when it needs to be poured into the pan (or in this case, the mold). Cold-process soap is the same thing—when it's ready to go, it needs to be poured in quickly before it sets up in the pot and becomes too thick. This is based on the chemical reaction between the fat and the lye, known as saponification. The recipes for cold-process soap are virtually infinite—the basic ingredients are lye and oil or fat, plus whatever "goodies" you want to add, such as fragrances, coloring, herbs, flower petals, and oatmeal.

Safety is a definite concern when making this type of soap. If you're working with novices or children, make melt-and-pour soap instead. Lye can be a dangerous chemical; it requires safety equipment and can give off fumes before it's added to the fat. Soap making is best done without distractions in a well-ventilated place, preferably without the "help" of pets or children who can cause spills or accidents. If you've never made lye-based soap, please read some basic articles or books about this process before attempting the recipe in this book.

This isn't intended to frighten you off from making your own soap, however. Once you're aware of the safety issues, have all your equipment ready, and are familiar with the process, soap making can be a fun and wildly addictive hobby, especially when you start experimenting with new recipes and ingredients.

As in the rest of the book, we start off with the simpler projects and work toward the more difficult or complex projects near the end of the chapter. If you're a complete novice to the idea of working with wax or making soap from scratch, start off by painting a candle, then carving a design into a candle, then explore a little bit of hot wax in the "Snow Candle" project. Once you're used to working with hot materials, it's an easy jump to play with melt-and-pour glycerin soaps and beeswax-based ointments. Now that you have a little more confidence, especially if you love to cook or enjoy candy making, take the next step into cold-process soap making. Like any new craft, you'll find it unfamiliar at first, and maybe you'll even put off trying it for months or years, but soon you'll make a new friend and proudly gift everyone you know with your own handmade soaps. In a short time, your knowledge and skill with candles and soaps might even turn into a small business venture! Give it a try, be safe, and have fun.

"MENDHI" PAINTED CANDLES

The painted designs in this project were inspired by the henna designs of India, called *mendhi*. These are painted on the skin with a reddish plant-based dye and were the original temporary tattoos, lasting a few days or weeks depending on how long the dried dye paste was allowed to sit on the skin.

YOU'LL NEED:

    White pillar candle
    Small folded towel to cradle candle
    Pin with a large head, like a T-pin or glass-head sewing pin
    Paper plate or pallette
    Toothpick
    Acrylic craft paint in dark brick red
    Candle medium
    #1 round paint brush or fine-tip applicator bottle

Set the candle on the towel and lay the pattern on top of the candle. Use the pin to lightly prick through the paper and into the wax to mark out the pattern of dots that makes up the mendhi design. Remove the pattern. Even if every dot is not distinct, it will show you where the pattern goes.

On the paper plate, using the toothpick, mix the paint and the candle medium according to the instructions on the bottle of medium. Load up the paintbrush with plenty of paint mixture or fill your fine-tip applicator bottle. Following the pattern of dots, make tiny dots of paint to create the design on the candle's surface. You may want to practice getting your dots even on the plate before starting on the candle. Also, the pin pricks in the wax may distort your perfect dots, so try to get the tip of the brush right in the holes. This will also help the paint to bond to the wax more securely.

Work small sections at a time, allowing the paint to set up or dry before turning the candle so that the dots stay perfectly round. When the finished portions of the candle are ready to be turned so they touch the towel, allow the paint to dry completely before continuing, which can be up to an hour depending on the temperature and humidity.

CELTIC CARVED CANDLE

Working carefully and slowly, it's easy to carve designs into colored candles. Make sure you get a candle that's been "overdipped," meaning a white candle that has been dipped into another wax color a few times. This is less expensive than making the entire candle out of colored wax, and normally considered a "cheap" candle, but this technique works to your advantage when you want to carve down and expose this white wax to make a beautiful design. Check the bottom of the candle or the wick to see if it's white underneath the color on the outside.

YOU'LL NEED:

> Dark-colored overdipped pillar candle (I used forest green)
> Small folded towel to cradle candle
> Ball-point pen or stylus
> Basic set of small wood-carving chisels

Lay the candle on the folded towel, which will act as a cushion and stop the candle from rolling as you work. Gently trace the pattern onto the candle by pressing on a photocopy with the pen or stylus. Don't press too hard or the surface of the candle could crack—if you press too lightly the design won't come through, however.

Use the small V-gouge to cut the outlines of the design. Use very gentle pressure and take your time—don't attempt to remove too much material at once or the colored wax could flake away. When the outlines are completed and white wax is showing in the grooves, use the shallow U-gouge to gently and carefully remove the colored wax between the lines. Periodically shake out the towel so that the discarded wax flakes don't stick to or scratch the candle's surface. Gently buff the surface of the candle if necessary to leave a nice finish.

"SNOW" CANDLES

I used to create these as a kid around the winter holidays, and they're really fun to make. It's amazing to see melted wax behave as if it's whipping cream! The secret to success here is to whip up only as much wax as you can apply in a minute or two, and to work lightly and quickly to maintain the "fluff" factor.

YOU'LL NEED:

A few ounces of plain paraffin
Metal coffee can
Old cooking pot
Large old mixing bowl
Old hand mixer
Cake decorating spatula or wide butter knife
White pillar candle
Small silver glitter (optional)

Place the paraffin in the coffee can, and place the can in the old pot. Fill the pot with about an inch of water to make a double boiler, and heat over medium until the wax is about half melted, then reduce heat to low. When the wax is melted, pour some of it into the old mixing bowl and whip it up with the old hand mixer until it's white and frothy.

Quickly, while it's still soft and partially melted, use the spatula or knife to "frost" the pillar candle with the frothy white wax. The wax will spread onto the candle base and stick to it because of the amount of partially melted wax in the froth. If the wax is too cold, it won't stick to the candle and will flake into little pieces. Keep whipping small new batches of melted wax and "frosting" the candle until it's completely covered with "snow." If desired, you can sprinkle a little dusting of silver glitter onto the candle while the snow is fresh enough to enable the glitter to stick to it.

BEESWAX OINTMENTS

Wortcunning, or herb lore, is one of the classic domains of the Witch. These gentle ointments can contain just the medicinal herbs you need for your situation using the basic instructions given here. This recipe is for a soothing itch relief balm that's good for all ages and skin types, and it's surprisingly easy to make.

You'll Need:

Small stainless steel cooking pot
1 tablespoon of dried comfrey leaves
¼ cup of dried calendula flowers
8 ounces of olive or almond oil
Mesh strainer
Small bowl
1 ounce of beeswax
Several drops of a gentle and relaxing essential oil, such as lavender, rose, or chamomile
Small heatproof plastic or metal ointment jar with lid

Combine the herbs and olive or almond oil in the pot and simmer over very low heat, uncovered, for about an hour, stirring occasionally. Pour the mixture through the strainer and into the bowl to remove the bulk of the dried herb material. Return the herbed oil to the pot, and add the beeswax. Simmer gently until the wax melts completely, stir in the essential oils and then pour the mixture into your ointment jar. Allow to cool completely. If you prefer the finished ointment to be firmer, re-melt and add a little more wax. If it's too thick for your tastes, re-melt the ointment and add another ounce of the same oil, then return it to the heatproof jar to cool once more.

MELT AND POUR SOAPS

Designer soaps are all the rage, and with good reason—they're easy to make and look fabulous! Glycerine is also especially good for those with sensitive skin, and contains no animal products (some cold-process soaps use lard and other animal fats). Most craft stores now stock the supplies for making your own "melt and pour" soap, and I'll bet that once you try it, all your friends and relatives will be getting handmade soaps for the holidays.

The Crafty Witch

   Melt and pour soap base
   Large glass measuring cup
   Microwave oven
   Colorants
   Spoon or stirring stick
   Fragrance oils
   Additives (spices, herbs, honey, glitter, dried botanicals, etc.)
   Measuring spoons
   Cookie sheet and knife (optional, to make spirals)
   Loaf mold or individual molds

The basics of making this kind of soap are easy—you prepare the mold, melt the soap base, add your goodies, pour it into the mold, and take out the finished soap when it's done. I've given two kinds of soap recipes here for you to try: a sliced loaf with a spiral inside and an herbal honey bar that's individually molded. To begin either recipe, determine the size of your mold and how much soap base you will need. An easy way to do that is to fill your mold with water and then pour it into a measuring cup.

For the spiral loaf, melt a couple of ounces of soap base in the glass measuring cup by heating it for about 30 seconds in the microwave, then stir and check to see that it's completely melted, and heat again in 15-second intervals until it's all liquid. Add a few drops of a dark colorant, such as blue or purple, and stir it carefully to avoid getting air into your soap. Measure the length of your loaf mold and pour a rectangle of colored soap onto a cookie sheet that is the same length as your loaf mold. Allow to cool and solidify just enough that it can be handled but it is still warm and moldable. Cut the edges off the rectangle so that it is the exact length of the loaf mold and gently roll it into a large, loose spiral. Chill in the freezer for a few minutes, then lay the cold spiral into the loaf mold. Melt the rest of the soap base needed to fill the mold, stir in about ¼ ounce of fragrance oil, and pour this clear soap over your chilled spiral, tapping the mold on the counter to work out any air bubbles. Allow to cool, remove from the mold, slice, and the bars are ready to use.

To make the individual herbal soaps, determine how many you want to make, add up the amount of soap base needed, subtract about an ounce, and melt in the microwave (see above). For each bar (multiply amounts as needed), stir in 1 tablespoon of warmed honey, 1 tablespoon of the dried herbs you want to include, and about 6–10 drops of an essential fragrance oil of your choice—how much oil you add depends on the oil's strength and your personal tastes. Stir carefully and gently to avoid air bubbles. Pour the mixture into individual molds, allow to cool completely, and remove from mold.

If you have trouble removing the soaps from the molds, tap them into your hand firmly or run them under hot water for a few seconds.

HERBAL COLD-PROCESS SOAPS

Like magic, a few basic ingredients combine here to create old-time classic soap that has been made in one form or another for centuries. Use the basic recipe for a plain bar to use with laundry or pets, or add your favorite herbs and oils for an exotic creation perfect for gift giving.

Hitting the right moment of saponification, when the ingredients are fully combined and begin to thicken, is a bit tricky. Your first couple of batches may not turn out well, but don't give up! Like I said, it's a lot like making fudge—you'll know how to recognize that crucial moment that the batch goes from "too thin" to "too late!" Once you get the hang of when to pour it into the molds, the rest is easy.

The best part about making your own cold-process soap is that you can be as creative as you want! Experiment with different oils to get the type of bar you like; add fragrant oils for their medicinal or aromatherapy qualities; leave your soap smooth or add scrubby herbs for texture; make it a swirly color or leave it natural ivory; tint your batch a solid shade or add several colors at once for a rainbow effect. The possibilities are endless!

YOU'LL NEED:

Plastic or stainless steel heatproof container (a covered pitcher is ideal)
Flat digital kitchen scale with $\frac{1}{10}$-ounce measurements
Large glass measuring cup
7 ounces of water
3 ounces of lye
16 ounces of olive, corn, or hemp oil
6 ounces of coconut oil
Rubber gloves
Safety goggles
Plastic or stainless steel spoon
2 candy thermometers
Stainless steel pot that will be your dedicated "soap pot"
Stick mixer
About $\frac{1}{2}$ ounce of essential or fragrance oils (optional)
About $\frac{1}{2}$ cup of dried herbs (optional)
Rubber spatula
Soap mold(s)

This recipe makes a little over 2 pounds of soap. If you need to make more or less, there are many soap recipe calculators on the Internet and in soap making books. Determine the amount you will need to fill your mold(s) before starting!

Get all your ingredients out and have them handy, as some of the processes in soap making require fast timing—if you don't have your dried herbs ready to go at the moment you need them, your soap could set up and be ruined while you're off getting them.

First, you will need to make a lye solution. Place your empty heatproof container on the scale, zero it out so you know how much water to add, and pour in the right amount. Put on your gloves and goggles, then put the glass measuring cup on the scale and zero it again. Add your powdered lye carefully until you have the right amount in the cup. *Very carefully and slowly*, add the lye to the water, stirring gently with the spoon.

Never add the water to the lye!! This can cause a violent chemical reaction that gets caustic lye everywhere! As long as you add the lye to the water, this will not happen and you're safe. A friend of mine made up a little poem to help remember which way to do this: "Add lye to water is what you ought'er . . . add water to lye and you might die." While you won't really die if you do it wrong, his poem is a good way to remember how to do the process safely.

When you add the lye to the water it will appear to boil and become very hot. Set the mixture aside to cool to about 100 degrees, keeping it covered in a safe place where it won't be disturbed or knocked over accidentally.

While the lye solution is cooling, pour your oils into your soap pot and begin warming them over medium-low heat, stirring occasionally. Prepare your soap mold(s) and have your other ingredients ready to go. When the oil mixture has reached about 100 degrees, and the lye mixture is about the same temperature, turn off the stove and slowly pour the lye mixture into the oil, stirring it with the spoon. Remember to carefully set aside your lye mixture container as the residue it contains is still highly caustic.

When you add the lye to the oil, the mixture will start to turn cloudy, which is the beginning of the chemical reaction known as saponification. Use the stick mixer to gently blend the ingredients well, but don't over-mix it or you will introduce too much air into your soap bars. When the mixture just barely begins to thicken, begin using your spoon to check for "trace."

This is when utensils begin to leave a line or mark across the surface of the mixture—to check for trace, dribble some of the liquid soap back into the pot and see if the drips stand on the surface for a couple of seconds before melting back in. Also see if your spoon or stick mixer is leaving a noticeable trail when moved through the thickening liquid. It's a little subjective, so use your best judgment and practice with your next few batches until you get just the thickness you want.

As soon as you hit trace, add your oils, botanicals, and colorants if desired. If you want a swirled color effect, add your colorants last and stir a few times with the spoon only—you can also try to swirl the color into the filled mold if you're using a large loaf mold. Another interesting effect is to sprinkle your botanicals on top of a loaf mold rather than stirring them throughout the soap. Oils, however, must be mixed into the soap base completely.

When these ingredients have been added to your satisfaction, pour the mixture into your soap mold(s), scraping out the pot with the spatula. Tap the mold(s) on the counter to remove any trapped air bubbles. Now place your curing soap, which will heat up as the chemical reaction continues, in a warm place such as a gas oven with a pilot light or the top of your fridge. Your soap will take about 24 hours to harden to the point that you can unmold or cut your bars, and they should cure for several weeks before use so that the saponification process is completed and any harsh qualities of the lye have been completely neutralized.

RESOURCES

General Wax & Candle Co.
P.O. Box 9398
North Hollywood, CA 91609
(800) 929-7867; candles.genwax.com

Wax, molds, dye, wicking . . . everything you need to make your own candles. If you're ever in the North Hollywood area, visit their outlet store at 6863 Beck Avenue.

Majestic Mountain Sage
918 West 700 North, Suite 104
Logan, UT 84321
(435) 755-0863; www.thesage.com

Fantastic resource for making cold-process and other forms of soaps, lotions, and more. If you've never made soap before, especially check out their complete kits! They also have online ingredient calculators and soap recipes, all for free.

Snowdrift Farm

2750 South 4th Avenue, Suites 107 & 108

Tucson, Arizona 85713

(888) 999-6950; www.snowdriftfarm.com

A very complete resource for the home soap maker, and one of the few places I've found that sells and ships lye. Their website also has many other supplies for making body care products and cosmetics, plus free instructional articles and chat groups.

Soap Crafters Co.

2944 S. West Temple

Salt Lake City, UT 84115

(801) 484-5121; www.soapcrafters.com

Loads of supplies and equipment for the home soap and lotion maker, including cruelty-free bases, pH papers, scales, stick blenders, molds, colors, scents, and embeddables.

The Soap Goat

P.O. Box 2792

Sumas, WA 98295-2792; www.thesoapgoat.com

A wonderful selection of Pagan, Celtic, Wiccan, and Egyptian soap molds, as well as loads of other molds and everything you need to make your own melt and pour soap. This is one of the best resources for the Pagan soap maker!

Wicks & Wax

3072 Beta Avenue

Burnaby, B.C., V5G 4K4, Canada

(800) 940-1232; www.wicksandwax.com

This complete company has beeswax, ointment containers, candle making supplies, and soap making supplies all in one place. They also sell wholesale for those who want to make a lot of soap, candles, ointments, or body/bath items for sale.

Fauna

As a vegetarian, I had a difficult decision to make regarding this chapter. Some readers criticized the "Fauna" chapter in my previous book. So when I began writing this book I had a talk with myself about including a chapter centered around the use of animal products in craft projects.

Why did the chapter win? Because even though I agree with the philosophies of vegans (those who use no animal products whatsoever) and vegetarians like myself (who don't eat meat), I decided that it wasn't up to me to limit the choices of others. Many vegans and vegetarians won't ingest animal products, but they wear leather shoes or use makeup (much of which is made with animal products), or wear jewelry made with seashells.

It basically comes down to personal choice, which is a huge grey area. If you're against using any animal product whatsoever, ignore this chapter. But maybe you're okay with using things like naturally shed feathers and things you can personally take responsibility for, or maybe you're happy to ignore the origins of where that leather came from and just wish to get out of all this preaching so that you can get to the projects. Don't worry, we're almost there.

If you're concerned about it, ask your leather supplier where the leather is coming from and request that they buy only from cruelty-free sources that treat their animals well and kill them quickly and humanely. Another alternative is to find secondhand supplies at flea markets, thrift stores, yard sales, from taxidermy students, and from friends. A more icky but free source of some materials, such as porcupine quills and rattlesnake rattles, is road kill. Check your local laws to see if it's legal to take road kill home with you . . . and make sure your partner is okay with a flattened animal in your freezer!

Another reason to keep a chapter like this in a book of Pagan crafts is the ancient tradition of using animal products in ritual items. To ignore the fact that all our ancestors honored these animals and used them in the past during sacred rituals is to do all of them a disservice. The four-leggeds, the wingeds, the swimmers, those that crawl on their bellies—all have their own sacred energies and these are still found in the physical remains they leave behind. Considering how many animals are annually shot and poisoned as "pests," how much beef and chicken is made into fast-food junk, how many animals are killed on our roads without a second glance . . . it seems to me that it honors their spirits far more to make sacred tools from their leather, feathers, shells, furs, quills, and rattles.

Techniques covered in this chapter encompass both the modern and the ancient, and ideas in between, too. Some simple leather work starts things off, then we move into some quick and easy tooling, followed by a unique rattlesnake rattle that seems difficult to make but is actually surprisingly easy. More complicated leather tooling follows, then some wet leather sculpting, and finally the most difficult project in the chapter, which is made with dyed porcupine quills. If you've never done quillwork before, this traditional Native American skill will truly test your crafting ability!

Some of these methods require specialized tools, especially the leather tooling projects like the Athenian Coin Book Cover. Most, however, use basic things you probably already have on hand (glue gun, wire cutters, various needles, a spoon, a pencil sharpener, and so on). That makes it easier for people who haven't done much leather work to get their feet wet and see if they want to do more before investing in the needed tools.

DECORATED LEATHER PET COLLAR

A new and hot area of crafting right now is making things for pets. Sewn carrying purses, homemade dog sweaters, bejeweled collars, and even yarn made with spun pet hair are all the rage, and why not? Our animal companions deserve a few goodies, too, like this decorated leather collar.

You'll Need:

    Raw leather pet collar kit
    Small leather punch
    Red (or your preference) acrylic craft paint
    ½-inch paint brush
    Leather clear coat
    Wool dauber

The Crafty Witch

Silver and black (or your choice of colors)
Kreinik metallic ¹⁄₁₆-inch ribbon
Tapestry needle
Needle-nose pliers
8- or 10-mm silver-tone jump rings or split rings
Assorted pewter charms

Punch holes along the center of the collar and along the edge as shown. Paint the collar, including the edges, and allow to dry completely. Cover with clear coat using the wool dauber and allow to dry completely.

Stitch one of the colors of Kreinik ribbon in and out of the holes in the middle of the collar until you reach the end. Either make a large knot at the beginning end of the ribbon or leave a 3-inch tail. Now take the second color of ribbon and either make a large knot at the end as before or tie the end to the tail of the first color. Stitch this color in and out of the opposite holes in the collar, giving you a row of alternate colors of ribbon running along the collar. Tie off on the back.

In the holes along the edge, use the jump rings (if a small animal) or split rings (if a large animal) to securely attach the charms to the collar.

TOOLED LEATHER PONYTAIL HOLDER

If you've never done leather tooling before, this small and easy project is a good place to learn. You can also try painting the motifs instead of staining it before applying the clear super sheen finish.

You'll Need:

Small scrap of 3–4 ounces or 5–6 ounces of tooling leather
Carbon paper
Leather shears or heavy scissors
Stylus
Swivel knife
Tooling stamps: B198, B199, C431, F976
Tooling mallet
Leather highlighter stain
Wool daubers
Moist paper towel
Leather clear coat finish
5-inch length of ¼-inch diameter dowel

Transfer the outline of the design onto the dry leather with the carbon paper and cut it out. Punch the holes for the dowel stick as shown.

Dampen the leather by running it under water briefly until it changes color—not too wet or the leather will be rubbery . . . too dry and it will be hard to tool. Use the stylus to press the design onto the wet leather, then use the swivel knife to cut carefully along the indented lines. To use a swivel knife, lay your index finger in the cradle at the top and use your thumb and middle finger to guide the knife around the curves. Hold it as vertical as possible so that you don't undercut the lines, then slightly tip the knife so that the corner can cut smoothly. For tight corners, you may find it easier to pivot the leather rather than the knife—if you're a beginner, try practicing on a scrap before cutting into your actual piece.

After all the lines are cut, use the beveller stamps along the cuts to depress the leather and create a three-dimensional effect with shading. Tap them gently but firmly, overlapping the stamps as needed for a smooth and even texture. Use the crescent-shaped C431 stamp for the top of the goddess's head.

Brush the finished design with highlighter stain and wipe off the extra with the damp paper towel. When the piece is dry, seal it with the clear sealer. To use the holder, make a point at one end of the dowel with a pencil sharpener so that it slides through easily.

RATTLESNAKE RATTLE

You'll have no trouble raising snake power with this unique rattle. The extra-long handle enables you to shake it harder so that the rattles really get buzzing. Use more rattles than you think you need—they're surprisingly quiet when not on the end of a snake!

YOU'LL NEED:

Several rattlesnake rattles (the example uses 4, more is even better)

11-inch length of ½-inch wooden dowel

Suede leather strips, approx. ½-inch wide (I used red and brown)

Low-temperature glue gun

1 yard of 26-gauge craft wire

Assorted glass seed beads (I used #11 red white-hearts and metallic copper)

Wire cutters

Trim the rattles if needed so that you have a clean, solid end to glue onto the dowel. Wrap the leather strips around the dowel, tucking under and gluing down the ends as needed.

Lay out your arrangement of rattles, then glue them in place to one end of the dowel. I placed the largest rattle on the very end, then surrounded it with smaller rattles placed on the sides of the dowel. Wrap the rattles with leather strips to cover the raw ends and help join them to the rest of the handle. Use glue as needed to secure them. If you used a contrasting color to wrap the rattles, add a strip of this color at the opposite end of the handle and glue down the end so it won't come loose.

Twist and wrap one end of the craft wire where the leather wrapping the rattles meets the handle. Thread an alternating pattern of four brown and four red beads (or the colors you chose) onto the wire until you have enough beads to wrap around the handle four times. You can change the pattern if you like, but this one honors the four directions and adds a bit of shimmer and color to your rattle. When you have enough beads threaded on, wrap the wire clockwise and then secure the end by twisting and wrapping it with the starting wire. Clip the end and tuck it underneath the bead strands.

TOOLED LEATHER ATHENIAN COIN PAPERBACK COVER

Just like two sides of a coin, you have two sides to this book cover, too! Copied from an ancient Greek Athenian coin, this design features the profile of the goddess Athena and her owl of wisdom as shown on the reverse.

YOU'LL NEED:

2–3 ounces of tooling leather, about 1½ square feet or larger
Small ball-tip stylus or blunt pencil
Swivel knife
Tooling mallet
Leather stamps: A104, B198, B199, B936, F976, H360, S724
Small leather punch or lacing stamp
Leather antiquing stain (optional)
Leather clear coat
Wool daubers
Small leather hole punch
Lacing

Cut the leather into 1, 7½-inch × 10-inch rectangle and 2, 2¾-inch × 7½-inch rectangles. This size will fit a regular small paperback—if you need a different size, open up the book flat on its spine and trace around it, then

add 1 inch all the way around for the basic cover. Scale the two inner flaps to fit, and scale the carving pattern as well.

Dampen the larger rectangle by quickly running it under the tap until it changes color. Don't get it too wet or it will be rubbery and difficult to work. When it begins to lighten in color slightly, add a bit more water as needed to keep moist as you work.

Use the stylus or blunt pencil to trace the pattern, pressing firmly into the surface of the leather to create an impression of the lines. If you prefer, you can switch the positions of the owl and the face. Using the swivel knife, follow these impression lines to carve the basic pattern into the leather. Stamp the design as shown on the pattern, using the photograph as an additional guide.

If desired, you can darken the piece with the antiquing stain, or you can simply cover it with clear coat and allow it to darken naturally over time. Stain and/or coat the other two pieces as well so that they are the same color as the cover. Matching the cover and the smaller rectangles that form the inner flaps, punch lacing holes as shown on the pattern. Grain (fuzzy) sides together, use a simple overcast lacing stitch to attach the flaps to the finished cover.

SHAPED LEATHER CAT MASK

If you have cats, you have access to the perfect finishing touch for this mask—whiskers! My four cats are constantly losing whiskers on the floor, in the clean laundry pile, on the sofa . . . anywhere the cats like to hang out. If you can't get cat whiskers, short lengths of medium-weight nylon fishing line work pretty well, too.

YOU'LL NEED:

9-inch × 12-inch piece of 2–3 ounces tooling leather
Pencil or stylus
Leather shears or heavy kitchen scissors
Plastic mask form
Bone burnishing tool or blunt clay modeling tools
Towel
X-Acto knife
Leather punch
Acrylic craft paints in brown, black, ivory, and dark rose
#1 and #6 round paint brushes
Leather clear coat
Wool dauber
Small craft drill, also called "pin drill"

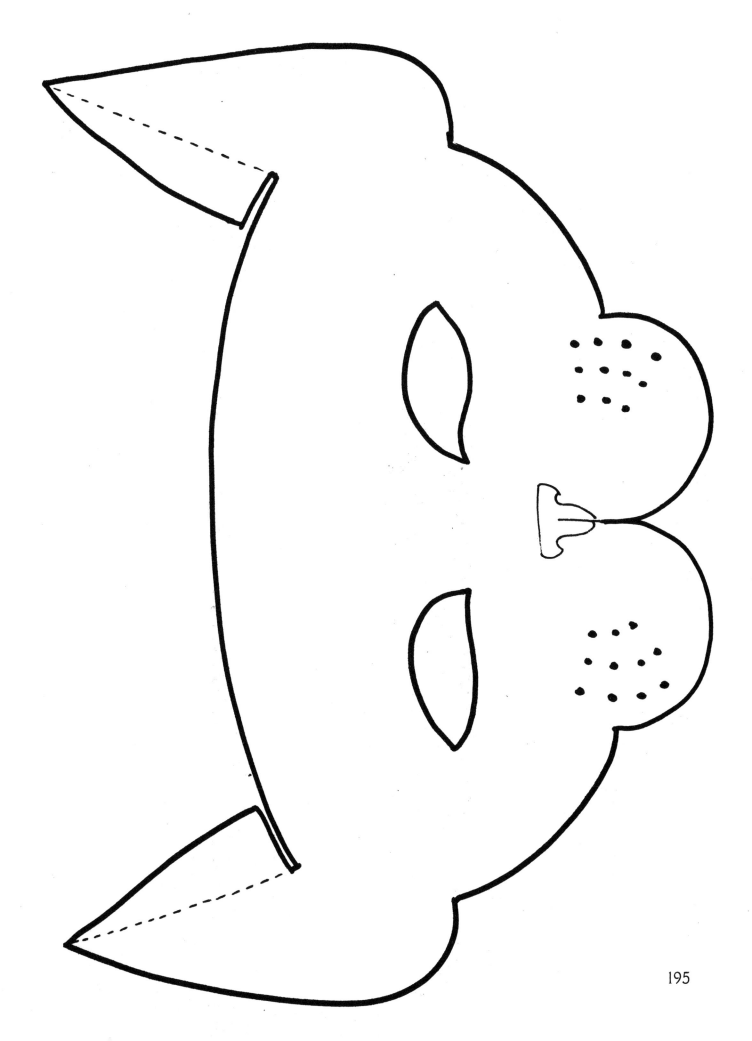

Cat whiskers or 3-inch lengths of medium fishing line
Tacky craft glue
Scraps of rabbit fur
Fine embroidery scissors
4 feet of leather thong

Thoroughly wet the leather and manipulate it to help break up the grain a little bit, resulting in a softer leather. Stretch, twist, and pull it until the leather is very soft and malleable. When you're finished, soak up excess water, and trace the mask outline into the wet leather with the pencil or stylus. Cut out the mask blank on this indented line. Do not cut out the eye holes yet.

Lay the towel down on your work surface, place the plastic mask form on top of it, and wet the leather again as needed. Lay the wet leather on top of the mask form, and use the burnishing tool and your fingers to mold and shape the leather to the mask form. Push it firmly into the corners of the form, using a balled-up towel under the mask form to help support it as necessary. Keep working the leather until it conforms to the face shape of the form, then fold over the ears as shown on the pattern. Allow the leather to dry completely on the form.

Using the X-Acto knife, cut out the eyes to fit your face so that you can see through the mask, and use the leather punch to make the nostril holes in the nose. Paint the cat's markings on the raw leather as shown on the pattern using the larger #6 brush for bigger markings and the smaller #1 brush for detailed work. When the paint is completely dry, use the wool dauber to apply the clear coat sealer over the entire front of the mask.

When the clear coat is completely dry, drill whisker holes as shown on the pattern. Dip the base of each whisker or length of fishing line into a dot of glue and firmly insert them into the whisker holes. If you're using real whiskers, be sure to use the longer ones closer to the sides of the face, and the shorter ones closer to the nose for a realistic effect. You can also trim the fishing line to get a similar effect.

Cut 2, ½-inch × 2-inch tapered strips of rabbit fur, making sure that the fur lays the right direction according to the illustration. Dot a little glue on the backs of the fur strips and tuck them inside each ear. Cut the thong into 4 equal 1-foot lengths. Punch 2 holes in each side of the mask and tie the 4 thong lengths in the holes, making 2 laces so that you can wear the mask comfortably.

PORCUPINE QUILL OAK LEAF DESIGN

Quillwork is a difficult and nearly lost art. It originated with the natives of North America as a way to decorate clothing and other items, but when traders brought colorful seed beads, which were more durable and easier to apply, quillwork quickly lost favor. A few artisans have preserved and are continuing this unique skill, however, and it's an interesting craft to attempt if you're skilled with a needle and patient with other detailed work. This oak leaf design can be done in any color combination you like, and the finished quillwork can be made into a pouch, moccasins, and so on.

YOU'LL NEED:

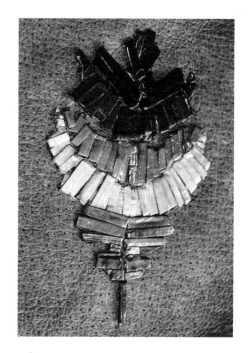

- 12-inch square piece (or desired size) of 2–3 ounces garment leather
- Masking tape
- Copy of the pattern
- 005 or 01 Sakura Pigma Micron permanent pen
- Dyed porky quills in green, yellow, orange, red, and purple
- Embroidery scissors
- Paper towel
- Several small dishes or bowls
- John James #12 beading needles
- Artificial sinew, split very fine
- Fine-tip pliers (optional)
- Spoon
- Several stacked sheets of blank paper
- Needle-tip tweezers

The garment leather should be supple, and should have suede on one side (fuzzy leather, also known as the "flesh side") and a smoother (but not hard and shiny) grain on the other side. Your needles will be slipped under this surface grain to hold the stitches, so suede won't work unless you can find a good braintan deerskin.

Cover the back of the leather with masking tape where the design will be stitched—this keeps the leather from stretching. Transfer the leaf design to the leather by making a copy, cutting it out just inside the outline, and tracing around it with the Sakura pen. Be accurate since you will be stitching on this line.

Sort the quills and look for good quillwork sizes. You want quills that are medium thickness—save the very fat ones for earrings, and use the very thin ones for fine work when you gain more experience. Ideal quills should be about 1 mm in thickness and as long as possible.

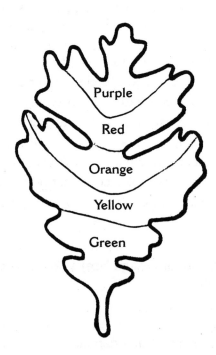

Porcupine Quill Oak Leaf Pattern

Carefully clip both ends off the quills by setting the point of the scissors where you will be clipping, then pinch the area with your fingers as you cut to catch the sharp tips. You do *not* want to lose the tip of a quill on the floor and find it later with your bare feet! The black tip in particular has barbs and will be extremely painful and difficult to remove, so always dispose of discarded quill tips carefully.

Fold the paper towel to about a 4-inch square and place it in one of your dishes. Moisten it with hot water and place several green quills on the towel, folding it over them to surround the quills with warm water. Let soak for about 2 minutes.

While the quills are soaking, thread two needles with the sinew, which should be as fine as sewing thread. Inside the border of the design, about a half inch away from where you will begin stitching, take a couple of backstitches just under the grain of the leather and then slide the needle over to the starting point of where you will begin stitching. Do the same for the second needle. On the bottom of the design (edge closest to you), take a 1-mm backstitch and leave about a half inch loop to start your first quill.

Check the quills to see if they're ready to be flattened. Lay a quill on the stack of papers and use the spoon (your quill flattener, which would have been an antler tip originally) to press gently into the quill. If you

The Crafty Witch

hear/feel a small "crunch," they're still too dry and need to soak another minute or so. If you slide the spoon down the quill and it doesn't seem to want to flatten, it's soaked up too much moisture and needs to set aside and dry a bit. The perfect quill should flatten easily and smoothly by drawing the spoon down its length. It shouldn't be puffy, puckery, or split. When the moisture level is right with your quills, take them out of the towel and set them aside so they don't continue to soak—put them in the towel as needed while you work to keep the moisture level just right.

With the black end toward you, lay the other end in the ½-inch loop you made with about ⅛ inch or 3/16 inch in the loop. Pull the thread tight and fold the quill up toward the opposite thread. Make another loop with the upper thread, this one about an inch. Loop it around the quill as shown in the drawing and gently draw it down to the leather. As you tighten the thread, use the needle-tip tweezers to carefully fold the quill under itself and down, and allow the loop to slip onto this back fold so that it stitches down the quill invisibly. To help align the quill, pull the two threads opposite each other (pull the top one up and the bottom one down), and also pull the upper thread and end of the quill opposite each other so that everything snugs up and lays properly.

If the quill is long enough, take another backstitch on the bottom line to secure it and fold it up again, repeating the top loop technique to continue the stitching method back and forth between the bottom and top lines. When you run out of quill, end it with a top loop as if continuing the pattern and clip off the extra so that the remaining black tail is hidden beneath the finished quillwork. Add a new quill just like you began the work, by securing the end of a flattened quill with the bottom backstitch.

Curving the work is a bit tricky, so don't be too frustrated if it doesn't lay the way you want the first time. Leave a slight gap between the quills on the outside of a curve and overlap them slightly on the inside of a curve. If you need to remove a quill, take the thread out of the needle and pull it back through to carefully release the quill. You can re-soak the quill for a short time, flatten it, and use it again elsewhere. If at any time your work wants to loosen up on you, simply take a small backstitch or two and this will prevent the thread from working loose. Another technique for crisp top and bottom edges is to use the spoon to flatten the edges of the quill while it is still slightly moist and sewn in place—don't try this when they're dry and brittle or they could crack.

Continue working toward the tip of the leaf, adjusting the stitching as needed so the quills will lay where you want. Work up and over the tip, continuing down the other side. The last quill will be the green stem, which is laid as one individual quill with the ends hidden beneath it. If any quills have come loose, whether because of leather failure or because the ends have slipped out of their stitching, feel free to go back and secure them so that you have a more durable finished piece.

RESOURCES

Claw, Antler & Hide Company
735 Mount Rushmore Road
Custer, SD 57730
(605) 673-4345; www.clawantlerhide.com

This company has things not found elsewhere, including just about any kind of bone, claw, horn, skull, or fur you could possibly need.

Crazy Crow Trading Post
P.O. Box 847
Pottsboro, TX 75076
(800) 786-6210; www.crazycrow.com

In business since 1970, one of the largest suppliers of Native American Indian and American Mountain Man items, craft supplies, and craft kits in the world. Be sure to check out their monthly specials, too.

Springfield Leather Co.
1463 S. Glenstone Avenue
Springfield, MO 65808
(800) 668-8518; www.springfieldleather.com

With a good basic selection and an amusing website, this is the place to get your leather. Springfield Leather will cut as much or as little leather as you need—you don't have to buy an entire side split here!

Tandy Leather
P.O. Box 791
Ft. Worth, TX 76101
(800) 433-3201; www.tandyleather.com

In the leather hobby business for many years, these guys have perhaps the best selection of bevel and pattern stamps for tooled leather, plus all the other supplies you need. Check out their starter sets if you don't yet have tools or need to expand your selection of stamps.

The Wandering Bull
P.O. Box 1075
Attleboro, MA 02703
(800) 430-BULL [2855]; store.wanderingbull.com

A good selection of porcupine quills, both dyed and undyed, and instructional books as well as many other native goods and supplies. Be aware that their dyed quill assortment contains about one-quarter undyed (white) quills, which might be fine depending on the design you're making.

ABOUT THE AUTHOR

Willow Polson is a born and raised Californian, and she has been a self-initiated Witch since the age of 13, receiving formal Priestess ordination in 2001. Willow has enjoyed writing and fiddling with all manner of arts and crafts since she was a little girl, especially embroidery. Her original goal was to become a high school art teacher, but when money for college became too scarce in her junior year at SFSU, she found an open door at a publishing company instead and jumped through.

Willow is one of the co-creators of *Veggie Life* magazine, and has been on the staff of other internationally popular magazines, including *Needlepoint Plus*, *Tole World*, and *Popular Woodworking*. Her own publishing venture, *Recreating History* magazine, featured articles on historic crafts, period foods, and how to be a better historic re-enactor. Lectures and featured appearances have included Pantheacon, Elderflower Womenspirit Festival, and several central California Pagan Pride Day celebrations. She is currently a member of the Embroiderers Guild of America (EGA) and the Society for Creative Anachronism's West Kingdom Needleworker's Guild.

For further info, tips, news, craft ideas, supplies and more, please visit www.willowsplace.com.